GIRLFRIEND,
IT'S YOUR TIME!

GIRLFRIEND, IT'S YOUR TIME!

Reclaim Your Brilliance and Step Into Your Purpose

TAI GOODWIN

WESTBOW
PRESS
A DIVISION OF THOMAS NELSON
& ZONDERVAN

Copyright © 2014 Tai Goodwin.

All rights reserved. No part of this book may be used or reproduced by any means, graphic, electronic, or mechanical, including photocopying, recording, taping or by any information storage retrieval system without the written permission of the publisher except in the case of brief quotations embodied in critical articles and reviews.

"While personal stories shared were inspired by true events, my recollections may not coincide with what others experienced or remember. Therefore, in consideration of that fact and in the interest of protecting their privacy, I have changed names, locations, and situations. Any resemblance to actual persons, living or dead, events, or locales is entirely coincidental."

THE HOLY BIBLE, NEW INTERNATIONAL VERSION®, NIV® Copyright © 1973, 1978, 1984, 2011 by Biblica, Inc.® Used by permission. All rights reserved worldwide.

WestBow Press books may be ordered through booksellers or by contacting:

WestBow Press
A Division of Thomas Nelson & Zondervan
1663 Liberty Drive
Bloomington, IN 47403
www.westbowpress.com
1 (866) 928-1240

Because of the dynamic nature of the Internet, any web addresses or links contained in this book may have changed since publication and may no longer be valid. The views expressed in this work are solely those of the author and do not necessarily reflect the views of the publisher, and the publisher hereby disclaims any responsibility for them.

Any people depicted in stock imagery provided by Thinkstock are models, and such images are being used for illustrative purposes only.
Certain stock imagery © Thinkstock.

ISBN: 978-1-4908-5357-4 (sc)
ISBN: 978-1-4908-5358-1 (hc)
ISBN: 978-1-4908-5406-9 (e)

Library of Congress Control Number: 2014917313

Printed in the United States of America.

WestBow Press rev. date: 11/26/2014

This book is dedicated to every heart brave enough to acknowledge the passion-based purpose they've been given, the lesson they've been called to live, or the message they have been divinely positioned to deliver…

…and to Shayna. You are the catalyst that ignited my greatest shift. I love you with all my heart and thank God that He blessed me to be your mother.

"We pray for the big things and forget to give thanks for the ordinary, small (and yet really not small) gifts." — Dietrich Bonhoeffer

I make it a practice to remember the small (and yet really not small) gifts. My deepest gratitude to the following supporters of this project:

Joseph Kastens
Sharon Nickey
Dianne Daniels
Matt Mansfield
Nicole Fende
Gail Roddy
M. Shannon Hernandez
Betty Liedtke

And extra special thanks to Melanie Keveles, my coach and confidant, who sent me daily messages prompting me to keep working on this. Love and light to you!

TABLE OF CONTENTS

Introduction ix
My Story xiii
The Truth About Brilliance 1
    The Impact of Eclipse Living 2
    You Always Have the Power to Choose 6
    It's Never Too Late to Pursue Your Purpose-Based Passion 7

Part I
Step Into Your Purpose 11

1 - Decide That Your Purpose is Not an Option – It's Your
    Calling 13
    Is Success More Important Than Significance? 15
    Are You Trying to Be Without Becoming? 17
    Are You Confident in Your Calling? 18
2 - Transform the Pain of Your Past 21
    Are You Your Own Worst Enemy? 23
    Are You Playing the Blame Game? 26
    Is It Time to Change Your Inner Game? 27
3 - Be Honest About What You Want 30
    Are You Trying to Talk Yourself into What You Don't Want? .. 33
    Have You Defined Success in a Way That's Meaningful
    to You? 35
    Are You Avoiding Making Difficult Decisions? 36

4 - Start Asking Better Questions..39
    Are You Making Excuses or Looking for Opportunities? 42
    Forget About Everyone Else, What Are You Telling Yourself? ... 45
    How Do You Face Closed Doors? 46
5 - Change Your Perspective on Failure 50
    Are You Afraid of Failure? 52
    Do You Really Want to Be Successful? 54
    Are You Comparing or Celebrating? 56
6 - Give Yourself Permission to Soar..60
    Are You Allowing Other People's Expectations to
        Determine Your Path? 62
    What Are You Waiting For? 63
    Are You Drowning in Doubt or Flying in Faith? 66
7 - Connect and Collaborate with Brilliant Women 69
    Is Your Network Working For You or Against You? 69
    Are You Cat Woman or Wonder Woman? 73
    How Are You Guarding Your Heart? 76

Part II
Fuel for Your Journey 79

1 - Unmask Your Excuses... 81
2 - Take the Risks that Bring Reward.. 83
3 - Refuse to Give Up When You Encounter a Setback 87
4 - Be Happy for Other People's Success 90
5 - Commit to Pursuing Your Purpose 93

It's Time to Reclaim Your Brilliance..95
    Who's Waiting For You?..97
About the Author 99

INTRODUCTION

We live in a world and time where women, particularly young girls, have a better chance of being scarred and marred in their lives than they do of becoming the shining stars they were purposed to be.

It's easy to point a finger at the media: the images we see promote mere slithers of the depths of who we are as women, daughters, mothers, and sisters. Our music and movies reduce us to attractive parts while ignoring the fragmented whole of who we are. We could point our fingers at our educational system. We could blame our local and federal agencies that create more dead ends than real opportunities. We could even call out our spiritual leaders who preach faith and prosperity, but fail to serve faithfully those who cannot serve them.

However, we have a choice. We can point fingers, or we can extend our hands. Pointing fingers and attaching blame rarely solves any problems. When we extend our hands, we all win.

Extending our hands in praise and gratitude sets our hearts free from bitterness and fills us with the light of acceptance. Extending our hands to each other creates the support and boundaries we need to grow stronger and stand taller. And extending our hands to reach back and pull more women into the light gives us the power to change lives, change our communities, and change our world. This is how we use our brilliance for good.

To use our brilliance, though, we have to reclaim it. We have to be willing to face the skeletons in our closet. We have to be willing to seek out the treasure that lies in some of our most painful experiences. Instead of dwelling on the past and fears that shackle you to a life less than what you were created for, I invite you to step into your to purpose. It's time to refocus your attention, set new intentions, renew your faith, and develop the habits of mind that will help you break through the eclipse blocking your brilliance.

It was the brilliant Maya Angelou who said, "When you know better, you do better." After watching my life and the lives of so many women, I realized that many of us don't know better. Experience and disappointment have taught us to build high emotional walls to keep people out. We intended these walls to be a protective shelter; instead they keep us in the dark.

Brilliant women know better. They have broken through the eclipse and broken free from thoughts that kept them shackled to the past. So now they do better. The good news is that wherever you are in your life right now, when you know better, you too can choose to do better.

Here are some truths that brilliant women know:

- Their purpose is not an option; it's their calling.
- Their past does not define them or their future.
- The level of their success is in direct proportion to how honest they are about who they are and what they want.
- Asking better questions trumps complaining.
- Failure, missteps, and mistakes are just stepping-stones to their purpose.

- Complacency is more dangerous than fear.
- You will never win trying to run someone else's race.
- Together we are stronger; collaboration is key to changing the world.

If you are ready to reclaim your brilliance and step into your purpose, I'm in your corner. It is never too late – Girlfriend, It's Your Time!

MY STORY

I know what it's like to reclaim your brilliance.
I know what it is like to be redeemed and restored.
I am a living testimony that a glimpse of
your wholeness can spark healing.
I know what it is like to feel loved from the inside out.

Owning my truth frees me to be exactly
who I have been called to be.
Living my truth allows me to stand confidently in my brilliance.
Speaking my truth pries open doors so
others like me can find their way.

I also know what it is like to live a lie. To appear to
everyone else as if you are thriving and on top of the
world, but on the inside feel like you want to die because
the weight of your pain is crushing everything in you.

I know what it is like to wrestle with believing in a God that seems
more concerned about sin than saving you from your suffering.
I know what it is like to break.
I know what it is like to be broken.
I know what it is like to cry from the pit of your soul
and feel like you are alone in absolute darkness.

What I have sown in tears, I now reap the reward of knowing that my pain can be for someone else's gain. There are lessons I have lived and messages etched on my heart that I have been divinely positioned to deliver.

I have reclaimed my brilliance.

THE TRUTH ABOUT BRILLIANCE

We all have brilliant beginnings. Think back to when you were four years old, or think about a four-year-old child you know. I remember watching my daughter at this age and being amazed at how fearless she was. She would scribble on a page and rush to show me what she'd done as if it were the most amazingly brilliant work of art. She'd beam with excitement after telling the most unintelligible knock-knock joke. Pages of misspelled words were masterpieces even if she was the only one that could read them. In her mind (and in my eyes), she was brilliant. Believing in her own brilliance didn't take away from anyone else, nor did it require buy-in from an external source. Of course, it helped that she had a mom who nurtured her spirit, but I was simply reflecting back to her the light shining from her little soul.

We all start off with that brilliance. Then life happens and slowly that brilliance gets stripped away. We encounter people and circumstances that strip the light away from us. Abuse, divorce, bullying, verbal attacks, overly critical parents and family members, illness, accidents, and the loss of loved ones are just some of the life-changing events that can begin to dim our light. For many of us, there may be multiple things that negatively impact how we see ourselves and the world around us. However, given the right context and players in a situation, just one of those experiences is enough to lead us into an emotional and spiritual eclipse.

The Impact of Eclipse Living

During a partial solar eclipse, as more of the sun gets covered by the moon, the sky becomes dimmer and dimmer. The only light comes from the edges of the sun that aren't covered. The light around the edges of a partial solar eclipse is blindingly brilliant; looking at it can burn your retinas before you can blink. In a total eclipse, the sun is completely covered by the moon, which makes everything go dark and causes the temperature to drop. Eclipses (partial and full) are natural, occurring every so often. They are not meant to last for an extended period of time.

With each negative situation and experience we are exposed to, our brilliance – our light – is eclipsed. There are incidents that cause a partial eclipse. In those cases, our resilience allows us to bounce back quickly to our brilliant selves. Then there are major incidents that shatter our souls, eclipsing our brilliance until all that is left is a light around the edges. Some of us get good at focusing on the edges: we create the appearance that looks good on the outside, while inside there is a darkness crippling our soul.

When our resilience isn't enough to bring us back, we end up living in eclipse mode. With our brilliance blocked, we spend years frozen in place. Our dreams and hopes die. Nothing grows, and life becomes colorless and bland. In a total eclipse, we wander in the dark and are unable to see a way out. In a perpetual cycle of stumbling, we live from a place of doubt, fear, and frustration. Even if the images we project to the world (the edges of our brilliance) are bright, our personal and professional lives are often mired in chaos and subject to catastrophic emotional outbursts.

Partial eclipses that dim our light every now and then are an expected part of life. It's normal to experience loss, grief, doubt, frustration, and disappointment. It is even okay to find ourselves going through a total eclipse. That's to be expected when we have misinformation about who we are or what we really need to move forward. However, it is not okay for us to live in total eclipse for an extended period of time. Why? Because living in an eclipse doesn't just impact us, it impacts our family, our relationships, and even the way we show up in the world to live out our purpose.

When we are in eclipse mode, we tend to feed the darkness with fear and anger based on the stories we tell ourselves. Stories based on past eclipses that dimmed our light:

- My father/mother left me…I'm not worth staying with.
- I was abandoned and overlooked…I'm not good enough.
- I was told not to tell anyone…No one will listen to me.
- I was neglected…My needs and wants are not important.
- I was told I was ugly, fat, unwanted, stupid…I will never be acceptable.
- I was dumped, raped, cheated on…No one wants me.
- I never get what I want…Nothing good ever happens to me.
- I was lied to and tricked…I can't trust anyone.
- I was used and taken advantage of…People are out to get me.
- I'll never have or be what I really want.
- I always fail.
- I am unlovable.

In coaching, we call those underlying automatic commitments. A situation or opportunity comes up and our first thought, usually a subconscious thought, is that underlying commitment based on the faulty stories we've been telling ourselves.

Someone gets the opportunity you wanted, and the underlying thought is – I must not be good enough. A relationship you wanted ends and you feel that same rejection you felt when your mother or father left – triggering thoughts that you are unlovable. You get good news or something you really wanted, and you automatically get worried and anxious, expecting something "bad" to happen because your story says, "Nothing good ever happens to me."

So how can you break through the eclipse and reclaim your brilliance?

It starts by being aware of:

- The facts of what happened in the past,
- The truth about where you are now, and
- The opportunities you have to choose differently and better.

From 5th grade to 12 grade, I went to a magnet school for gifted students. To get in you had to either pass a test or be recommended by a teacher. My 4th-grade teacher recommended me. There were about five or six classes for each grade level until you got to the 10th grade. For high school, 10th -12th grade, there was just one class for each grade level. In the late 1990s, it was one of the top public high schools in the country. Even if you had been there since 5th grade, you had to apply to be allowed to stay for high school. I applied and was one of just 27 students accepted into the 10th grade that year. I was also the only African-American female student.

I spent my junior and senior years working about forty hours a week at a center city bookstore. I worked from 3:30 pm to 11:30 pm Wednesday through Sunday. Although I had to stop playing volleyball so I could work, I kept my grades up and was excited about graduating and going to college. Back then I wanted to be a broadcast journalist (like Oprah). After taking the PSATs, I began researching schools and came up with a list of schools I was interested in. Hofstra, Syracuse, and Boston University were at the top of my list.

When it was my turn to sit down with an advisor, I proudly bounced into Mrs. Kinsley's office with all of my research and application dates. She read my list, then looked me straight in the eyes and said, "I think you are reaching above yourself. You need to find something more on your level." Imagine hearing that from someone that was supposed to be helping you think about your future.

I was crushed. I felt embarrassed. I felt stupid. At that moment, I decided that I didn't want to go to college. In fact, I applied to only one school, and that was because my homeroom teacher, Mr. Gordon, made me. The expectation was that every graduate would go to college. So after studying AP Biology, Calculus, AP History, Spanish (level 4), and maintaining a B average while working 40 hours a week, I applied to Drexel University as a fashion design major. Not only did I get in, but I also earned a 3.6 GPA the first quarter, and a 4.0 my second quarter (our 'semesters' were just 10 weeks long), all while working a part-time job and work study.

On the outside, it looked like I was succeeding. On the inside, I was struggling: I was depressed, hurting, and in constant fear that I would fail. By the end of my second year, I dropped out. Eventually, I went back and finished with a degree in Education. However, the discouragement of that conversation with Mrs. Kinsley lingered in my soul and became another facet of the eclipse that blocked my brilliance.

It was years before I had the courage to tell anyone about that conversation with my advisor. Neither of my parents had been to college, and something in her words and the way she looked at me made me feel ashamed for wanting to go. Her voice added to that record played so often in my head that said, "Who do you think you are?"

Years after that encounter with Mrs. Kinsley, I still struggled to find the confidence to pursue what I really wanted. My breakthrough didn't come until I learned to distinguish between the facts and the truth of that experience. The facts are:

- Everyone is entitled to his or her opinion.
- My guidance counselor's opinion about who I was and what I was capable of was an inaccurate assessment of my potential.
- Because I didn't know any better at the time, I accepted her opinion as truth.

The truth is:

- I cannot change the past.
- That entire situation now fuels my passion for helping women and young girls.
- Right now I am exactly where I am supposed to be.

You may have a similar story. In fact, if you are like me you have had more than one experience with a misguided guide. No matter what or whom you have encountered in the past, you are exactly where you are supposed to be.

You Always Have the Power to Choose

- This second, someone will choose to complain, and someone else will choose to express gratitude.
- This minute, someone will choose to be bitter over a rejection, and someone else will choose to look for another door.
- This hour, someone will choose to let a past misstep cripple them, and someone else will choose to learn from yesterday's mistakes.

- This day, someone will intentionally choose to crush someone's dreams with their own fear and judgment, and someone else will purposely choose to sow into someone else's life.
- This week, someone will choose to quit and give up on pursuing their purpose-based passion, and someone else will choose to make resilience their habit and keep going no matter what.

A month, year, or decade from now we will all be living out the manifestation of the choices we make right now. It can be tempting to choose to quit, especially when so many people opt out and settle for mediocrity. Not everyone is supposed to be an entrepreneur. Not everyone is meant to write a book. Not everyone is called to speak to crowds of thousands and ignite change. But this isn't about everyone else. This is about you, your purpose, your passion, your vision, your calling, and the people you are meant to serve.

Right now, you need to make a choice. Will you settle for a life, relationships, and work that are beneath what you want and what you are capable of? Will you make mediocrity a friend and refuse to break connections to what doesn't serve your true purpose? Will you remain a disciplined wisher, spending hours fantasizing about your vision while sleeping your life away? Will you continue to live in fear – fear of what other people will say, fear of being seen as something other than successful, fear of failing, fear of being disappointed? Or, will you reclaim your brilliance and pursue your purpose?

It's Never Too Late to Pursue Your Purpose-Based Passion

"Destiny is no matter of chance. It is a matter of choice. It is not a thing to be waited for; it is a thing to be achieved." — William Jennings Bryan

No matter where you are right now, it is 100% possible to pursue your purpose-based passion and create prosperity that serves you and what you have been called to do. While it may seem hard to pursue your passion, it is much harder to live and work without it. If the prosperity you desire has always seemed to elude your grasp, you can start sowing different seeds today to bring about the harvest you want. If you are open and willing, your current situation is ripe with opportunity.

You may cross paths with people who will try to tell you that it's too late. Maybe you're telling yourself that it's too late. I want you to know that is simply not true. It's not too late to pursue your purpose: the people you were meant to serve are waiting for you to show up.

I have an aunt who has always loved interior design. In her 50+ years, she has raised three sons, homeschooled them for several years, been a day care provider, worked in accounting and as a social worker. She's amazingly resourceful, a fantastic artist, and a great teacher. Her track record is already impressive, right? So guess what she decided to do about five years ago? She decided to go back to school for a master's degree in interior design. She applied and got into one of the top programs in the Philadelphia area. It's been amazing to watch her pursue her passion and push past the challenges of:

- All of the students being younger than her
- Having to learn how to use AutoCad and Illustrator (complex design programs), even taking extra classes outside of the master's program so she could keep up
- The recession and a shrinking job market for interior designers
- Budget cuts that ended her full-time job as a social worker
- Three sons in college

She could have easily said it's too late. She could have easily said this is too hard. She could have stopped, and no one would have blamed her. I admire her tenacity. I admire the example she is setting for her children and my other cousins. Seeing my aunt boldly pursue her passion inspires me to pursue mine. As you step out to pursue your passion, who is looking to you as a role model?

From My Heart to Yours…

I pray that you begin to envision how different your life can be when you live from a place of knowing that your experiences, even the most painful ones, can be leveraged into a life-changing message for someone else. I pray that you begin to see the impact you will make once you wholeheartedly believe that embracing your truth is the key to fulfilling your purpose. I pray that you choose to take action. The world is waiting for you.

PART I
STEP INTO YOUR PURPOSE

1 - DECIDE THAT YOUR PURPOSE IS NOT AN OPTION – IT'S YOUR CALLING

Brilliant Women Know: Purpose is the key to contentment, abundance, and true prosperity.

Bright women try to quench their desire for purpose with material things, relationships, and external validation. No matter how much they acquire, they are never fulfilled. They believe that money is a way to have more meaning, when in reality it's meaning (their purpose, intention, and vision) that gives money any real value at all. There is a void in their heart and soul that longs for a deeper connection to their Creator and their purpose.

Hope deferred makes the heart sick, but a longing fulfilled is a tree of life. Proverb 13:12

The truth of these few words is what inspires me as a coach. I'd much rather help people create a tree of life stemming from their purpose-based passion than watch them become heartsick. I see heartsick people all the time, especially women who believe they have to put their dreams, purpose, and passion on hold. Marriage, children, finances, family, and a good job – all can become excuses that detour us into a carefully constructed crevice of mediocrity.

I've been in that crevice. Desperately yearning to find that place where purpose, passion, and prosperity are connected, but settling for two out of three. I had a good job, a good six-figure job, in fact, and I was doing something I enjoyed – designing and developing training programs. What was missing for me was a sense of purpose. I had an unrelenting desire to contribute in a way that had real meaning and impact, and was in alignment with my values.

For years, I stayed on a path that looked like success to others: I held positions at Fortune 500 companies, earned a six-figure income working as a remote employee, and received recognition and awards for my work. I spent years "looking" successful, but I was deeply unfulfilled. No matter how much makeup I wore, how many different ways I styled my hair, or how much money I spent on clothes, shoes, and jewelry, there was never any sense of purpose in how I spent 40+ hours of my week. I was unhappy, overworked, and frustrated. The suffering not only impacted me, but it had a ripple effect that influenced my daughter, my relationships, and even my connection with God.

Being disconnected from my purpose created a spiritual gap that I tried to fill with more money, bigger titles, increased responsibility, more recognition – but none of it worked. My performance at work was stellar, but my personal life was disastrous. It's one of the reasons I became a workaholic: at work, I knew how to make things happen. Outside of work, I had no clue how to break down my own walls so I could create and enjoy a healthy relationship with others or myself. The more I pursued things that took me in the opposite direction of my purpose, the more heartsick I became.

I was living in an eclipse, and any hope I had was deferred by settling for good enough. But…longing fulfilled is a tree of life.

I started building my business in 2008 while I still had a day job. In 2012, I officially stepped away from the paycheck and left the day job that was slowly killing my soul. Launching while working, and even transitioning from employee to full-time entrepreneur, is hard, but the reward is sweet. Nothing beats waking up every morning loving the work you do, knowing you are changing lives, and feeling a deeper connection to your creator every time you "work."

Is Success More Important Than Significance?

One of the reasons we put off pursuing our purpose and calling is that we are afraid of what we might lose. It's the brand or image you've worked so hard to build, but feel called to change. Maybe you've gotten accustomed to a set standard of living that you'll have to trade temporarily while you are investing in your vision. Or maybe, you'll have to let go of certain connections and relationships to make room for new environments and circles where you are not yet known. You could choose to hold onto the things that give you a feeling of success, but do they really matter if there's no significance to having them? What if true fulfillment is not just found in what we achieve, but in the significance of what we do?

Focusing on the objects of success, rather than the significance of our actions, creates a cycle of disappointment. We also miss the opportunity to sow into the lives of others. Instead of focusing on what you might have to give up or lose, focus on the lives you have the potential to impact. How many people are waiting for you to step into your purpose?

When your true self is a vibrant, passionate, ambitious professional – it is tremendously difficult to get enthused about doing work that dims your light. Even if you are good at what you do, are praised by the people in your circle, have a glamorous title, or bring home six-figures. If your soul is purposed to serve from another place, none of those things will satisfy you. It's why one more vacation, one more pair of shoes, one more relationship, or one more pay raise will never ever be enough.

Prosperity without purpose is meaningless.

Pursuing your purpose-based passion feeds not only your soul, but also the lives and souls of all the people you are meant to serve, whether it's through your speaking business, the web app you dream of designing, the clothing line you want to bring forth, or the book that runs through your mind every time you close your eyes. What's in you has the power to transform your life and the life of others.

"Sounds nice, BUT I've got responsibilities," you say. "There's no way I can go after what I really want to do. My passion will have to wait."

I counter that response by charging you to think about your responsibility to:

- Bring life to the vision you were given.
- Use the gifts and talents you were given.
- Serve the people you've been called to reach.
- Live authentically and with integrity.

We all have responsibilities. Having responsibilities is neither a reason nor an excuse for putting your purpose-based passion on the back burner.

Pay the bills, take care of your family, be an excellent wife and mother, AND find a way to pursue your purpose-based passion. Why? Hope deferred will make your heart sick. Not pursuing your passion can lead to depression, despondency, burn-out, bitterness, frustration, anger, and jealousy. It can also have an impact on you physically and spiritually as you look for substitute fulfillment in things that will never bring the peace and contentment you desire.

If your heart is sick because you have been putting off your purpose, the one person that can begin the healing process is you. If you have been waiting for a sign or message – this is it. You don't owe anyone else's expectation an explanation or rationale for pursuing your purpose. But you are dishonoring your gifts and the One who has given them to you when you ignore your calling.

Are You Trying to Be Without Becoming?

There's a line in a Christian rap song that goes, "…no one wants to become, they only want to be." For most people, our first exposure to someone who has "made it" occurs when they are at the "Be" stage of their career. We celebrate, praise, and in some cases idolize them based on the current image they present to the world.

But what about the less glorious phases of that person's path, the time they spent "becoming." We don't often get to see behind the scenes of their early years – the hours of practice or study, the rejection they encountered, the failures, disappointments, and the setbacks. We don't see the time and energy they diligently invested and the habits they worked hard to build over the years. If we were honest, many of us would admit that we don't really want to have to put in all the effort, but we do want the results. We want to "be" and we want it now!

Over time, it becomes easy to weed out those who jumped to the "be" phase without laying a good foundation. At the height of their careers when they should be flourishing, we see them floundering. Personality flaws and insecurities that were never addressed make for great entertainment news. Bad habits turn into self-destructive behavior that clearly illustrates they were trying to "be" someone they had not done the work to become.

Are you doing the work to actively cultivate the practices that will bring you long-term success? Or are you feverishly working to create an external image, which gives the appearance of "being" without the substance to back it up? Without a solid foundation and healthy habits, any adversity you encounter at work or in your business has the potential to derail you.

Habits are developed not by some magic enlightenment that suddenly makes us do the right thing. Habits, both good and bad, develop when we consistently make decisions to act in alignment with what we value.

Are You Confident in Your Calling?

I spent years basing my decisions on what other people said, what other people wanted, and what other people expected. I allowed their judgments, criticisms, prejudices, fears, and limitations to become the lens through which I saw myself. Not only was my vision of myself clouded, but opportunities and options were blurred beyond recognition, as well.

It's a hard road to walk when you are led by other people's agendas and fears. You will be tossed and turned like leaves blowing in the wind. They may be pretty to watch, but eventually they will get raked, piled, and discarded. But you, my dear, are meant for more! It's time to be confident in your calling. Confidence lets you:

- Dream big! You see potential opportunities instead of potential problems.
- Speak with authority. You can say what you want and ask for what you need.
- Choose wisely. You stop second-guessing your decisions or seeking validation from other people.
- Act boldly! You take steps to prepare for the success you expect.

The more you dream, speak, choose, and take action, the more your confidence grows. Conversely, inaction, indecision, negative self-talk, and focusing on what you don't have corrupts your confidence.

Don't bury your gifts and talents. Don't ignore the purpose you are meant to live out and the passion waiting to be ignited. Reclaim your brilliance and lead with your light! Let every decision you make, path you choose, and relationship you build be based on it. It's the only way to create authentic success. It's the way you will have more impact and influence. And it's the way you will increase your prosperity.

Leading with your light requires you to dream big. Small dreams won't adequately serve you or the people you were meant to serve. So dream big and bold! Practice seeing the results of pursuing your purpose — visualize the lives that will be changed and the impact you will have for years to come.

Are You Bright or Brilliant? Spend time reflecting on the following questions:
- Are you more focused on accolades and the appearance of success than living on purpose?
- How would your internal and external life change if you had clarity about your calling?
- What long-term impact would you have on the lives of others and your community if you were living on purpose?
- What stands in the way of your being more confident in your calling?

Step Into Your Purpose: Be Confident in Your Calling

1. See It: Get a clear picture of the people you were meant to serve and how your gifts, talents, and experiences can impact their lives.
2. Say It: Write down your vision and read it out loud to yourself once a week.
3. Share It: Don't keep this all to yourself. Tell five people about it. Make sure you share with your supporters. If you don't have any, you need to get some.

From My Heart to Yours...

Stop doubting yourself and questioning your heart's desires because of a lack of validation from other people. I pray that you value your purpose, talents, and potential too much to allow other people to nudge you off-course. There will be times when pursuing your purpose may make you feel alone. It is just part of your journey, part of the process that enables you to be your most brilliant. I pray that you have the courage to follow your path – even when others can't see it. Know that you have been equipped with everything you need.

2 - TRANSFORM THE PAIN OF YOUR PAST

Brilliant Women Know: The pain of their past can be an anchor or a catalyst.

Bright women reach a certain level of success and satisfaction, but are always pulled back into eclipse living by the pain of their past. Refusing to forgive themselves and others, they carry an anchor in their soul. This anchor only allows them to feel a certain level of freedom, lightness, and happiness before it snaps them back to darkness. Some of them learn to lengthen the chain, and sometimes they break through the eclipse a little before the chain attached to their anchor pulls them back down again. Their pattern of self-sabotage is stirred up by feelings that they are unworthy of having what they really want.

I have a lot of pain in my past. Most of my clients have some sort of pain in their past. In fact, most people who work in helping professions like teaching, coaching, and counseling have painful pasts. Our pain is often a driving factor in why we want to help others: we know what it's like to struggle, and have a deep desire to set others free.

When we see people suffering, something in our spirit connects to their pain and we want to help them. We are drawn to helping professions and roles because we realize that all the pain and hurt we've gone through has a bigger purpose: We can turn the lessons we've lived into a message that can spark healing and hope in others.

Sometimes the very pain that allows us to connect to others can be an anchor. It can weigh us down and keep us shackled to the past if we let it. We have a choice: we can either bury our pain in the back of our emotional closets like something we're ashamed of or we can learn to transform the pain of our past into a gift. Burying our pain keeps us attached to it in an unhealthy way. No matter what happens on the outside, we always know it's there. In fact, we often visit the back of the closet just to make sure it's still there, covered up and out of sight. We smile to the world, but as soon as our life slows down and we are alone, the pain consumes us.

If we learn to see the pain of our past as a gift, we get to wrap it with the lessons we've lived and gift it away to others. We allow them to be blessed by the very thing that attempted to break us.

One of the things buried in the back of my closet was the pain and shame of being molested when I was a very young girl. Growing up, my entire body was tense with holding that secret. I spent many of my younger years detached emotionally and physically. I had severe issues with self-esteem and developed a need to please other people regardless of what it would cost me. Most importantly, my relationship with God was distorted. I was angry because of what He "allowed" to happen to me. If He really loved me, I told myself, He would have intervened like He did for other people who had these amazing stories of escape and rescue.

For years, my pain served as an anchor; I believed I was worthless and damaged. The sting of shattered trust and being violated kept me chained to the back of my closet. Even with a bachelor's degree, a master's degree, a six-figure income, professional accolades, and the outside image of success, I realized I was just lengthening the chain. What I really needed to do was break it.

Through praying, self-work, and truth telling, I was able to break free from the anchor of pain weighing me down. I found a way to turn my pain into a gift, a story I could share with others to help them break free of their chains and break through the eclipse blocking their brilliance.

- Each time I share it with a woman who has experienced something similar, I am giving her a gift of hope and the promise of restoration.
- Each time I share my story at a speaking engagement, I am igniting the gifts of healing and forgiveness.
- Each time I show a client how their story can be incorporated into their message, I am helping them shift their pain into purpose.

My pain is now their gain.

Is the pain of your past serving as an anchor? Or have you figured out how it can be a catalyst for owning your truth and living your purpose?

Are You Your Own Worst Enemy?

"Believe in yourself and there will come a day when others will have no choice but to believe with you." — Cynthia Kersey

Finally! You get the perfect opportunity, the one that you've been waiting for. The thing that will put you in the perfect position to get what you really want. You get excited. You start imagining just how awesome everything is going to be. You tell everyone about this great opportunity that has landed at your feet. You start planning and preparing, doing the work to make the most of this open door.

And then you hear it.

It starts off as a whisper and steadily grows to a roar that fills your head with a hundred thoughts of why it will never work. Your light-hearted enthusiasm turns into a knot in your stomach and tension in your shoulders. Before you know it, you are at a familiar fork in the road. Both forks lead to your opportunity, but one path is lined with light, self-confidence, and self-love. The other path is dark, lined with pointy-edged criticisms and self-sabotage. The only problem is that it can be hard for you to see the difference until it's too late.

Here are five red flags that you are on a path to self-sabotage:

#1 - You set your expectations low. Settling for less than what you want means you stop short of unleashing your fullest potential. Maybe you settle for less to avoid the disappointment of failure. Other times, you settle only because you lack awareness of your own strength. Begin proving your strength by raising your expectations. Your own fear is often the biggest obstacle between you and your purpose. Instead of running from it, face it.

#2 - You feel sorry for yourself. If you feel like something is missing from your life or you are not getting what you want, do something about it. Instead of dwelling on what could have been, train yourself to see options and possible solutions. Instead of focusing on the unfortunate hand you've been dealt, look for the lessons you can learn. Own the truth that your success is your responsibility. Hold yourself accountable for the results you want and refuse to be deterred from pursuing your purpose.

#3 - You don't have a second plan. If your initial plan isn't working, don't give up – adapt. Everyone needs a Plan B. Keep in mind it's not the destination that's changing, but the plan for how to get there. You may feel like a pessimist by creating a back-up plan, but you are actually being proactive. Coming up with another way to reach your goals shows resilience and tenacity. It means you're serious about pursuing your purpose, no matter what.

#4 - You refuse to rely on your support system. Being independent, resourceful, and responsible is great. There's also value in knowing how to lean on others when you need to. You don't have to do everything alone. At the very least, you need cheerleaders to help drown out your inner gremlin and remind you that it is safe to dream big and live your purpose. If you know that self-sabotage is something that repeatedly creeps onto your path, ask your inner circle of supporters to be on the lookout for behaviors and old thinking that have the potential to take you off-course.

#5 - You're depending too much on others. It's great to have a support system. Just be careful not to make them your crutch. When you feel a sense of entitlement to help from others, or expect others to bail you out of a tough situation, you could be abusing your support system. Even if your friends and family have helped you in the past, they have the right and may choose to let you handle your own challenges and support you from a distance. Remember, ultimately you are responsible for your success.

The Solution: Stop Being Your Own Worst Enemy

Being aware of self-sabotaging behaviors is half the battle. Until you decide that you are capable of and deserving of success, YOU will continue to be the biggest hindrance to living your purpose. Want to avoid self-sabotage?

- Be conscious of the red flags listed above,
- Pay close attention to any fears you are holding on to about success, and

- Change your inner game by replacing "stinking thinking" with solution-oriented affirmations that better reflect your brilliance.

Are You Playing the Blame Game?

I love this quote by George Bernard Shaw: "People are always blaming their circumstances for what they are. The people who get on in this world are they who get up and look for the circumstances they want, and, if they can't find them, make them."

Are you reaping the benefits of blame? Deep down we know that blaming doesn't change the situation. But it is so easy to play the blame game and attribute the reason for our lack of progress to something or someone other than us.

Here are a few of the payoffs or benefits we get when we blame our circumstances or other people:

- We don't have to do anything. As long as it is some other person's fault or the action belongs to someone else, we don't have to do anything. We are free to procrastinate, daydream, remain passive, etc.
- We don't have to be responsible for our decisions or actions. Accountability is overrated anyway, right?
- We get to avoid failure. If it is not our fault, it is not our failure. And since we all know failure is the worst thing that could ever happen, we need to avoid that altogether.
- We get the pleasure of judging, labeling, and criticizing. Let's be honest, sometimes it feels really good to point a finger at someone else. It makes us feel like we are in control even though we know we're in the situation because taking control is what we failed to do.

Blaming seems like a pretty cool deal until you take off the blinders and acknowledge the consequence: Your actual accomplishments pale in comparison to your potential.

Whatever you attribute your failure or lack of progress to is what you are allowing to control your level of success. Your success, or failure, is not dependent on your circumstances. However, the impact and influence of your circumstances are totally dependent on your mindset, beliefs, and actions.

Is It Time to Change Your Inner Game?

Eventually, what you think on the inside gets reflected on the outside. You can spend time and money making your outer image spectacular. But the longer you go without repairing the inner cracks and holes behind the facade, the more damage you do to your soul.

Think of it like a thick pane of glass with a crack from the inside. No matter what you do to decorate and cover up the crack from the outside, it's still there. And not only does the crack get deeper and longer the more it remains unaddressed, it gets more fragile. On top of that, everybody can see it, despite your attempts to cover it up.

We see examples of this in our culture everyday:

- It's the millionaire movie star crippled by addiction, ruining her career.
- It's the beautiful model plagued by insecurity and jealousy, engaging in self-destructive behavior.
- It's the self-made businesswoman doubting her every move, always underestimating her true value.
- It's the six-figure corporate executive, leaving a trail of broken personal and professional relationships.

- It's you, the talented, driven, gifted woman with a vision, unable to create the success you see so many others having in work, business, and life.

If you never change your internal thoughts, your default patterns and behaviors will inevitably corrupt any progress you make towards pursuing your purpose. The remedy is to invest the time and energy in changing your inner game, so that your outer game is authentically brilliant.

Are You Bright or Brilliant? Spend time reflecting on the following questions:

- What lessons have you lived that can be used to help other women find forgiveness, restoration, healing, and hope?
- What red flags keep showing up in your path to indicate you are sabotaging yourself?
- What circumstances have you been blaming for your inability to move forward?
- What negative thoughts and self-talk do you need to address?

Step Into Your Purpose: Choose to break free from the pain of your past.

Now that you've identified the "anchors" that have been weighing you down, how can you use them as a catalyst for pursuing your purpose?

From My Heart to Yours…

I know what it's like to live shackled to the pain of your past. I also know the joy, freedom, and self-love that come from deciding to let that pain be a catalyst that ignites your brilliance. I pray that you forgive those who hurt you in the past, so you can move forward to the life you are being called to. I pray that you forgive yourself and learn to desire grace more than perfection. I pray that no matter how hard it feels, you will find strength and courage in knowing that your pain can be for someone else's gain.

3 - BE HONEST ABOUT WHAT YOU WANT

Brilliant Women Know: Their level of success is directly related to how honest they are about what they really want.

Bright women spend lots of time trying to mask an internal conflict. They lie to themselves and others about what they want and what they are worth. In some cases, they go through extreme measures to convince themselves and other people that they don't want or need anything. They have a hard time accepting praise and internalizing sincere validation and recognition from external sources. They have no problem giving praise to other people whom they think deserve it. But they are bothered by women who "toot their own horn" and take the lead without checking in with others first. They'll tell you they just don't like women who are showy or "pushy" – but what they really feel is envy towards women who do what they cannot: confidently ask for what they want.

If you are not true to yourself and the vision you have for your life, I can guarantee that disappointment and regret are contributing to your eclipse, blocking you from the success and fulfillment you really want.

You will never be content with success based on lies about what you really want.

I started lying to myself about what I really wanted in 4th grade. That's when I began to feel anxious and uncomfortable about being smart.

When I was in 3rd grade, I was placed in a 5th-grade reading class. At first I was excited about traveling to a 5th-grade class – they were the "big" kids on the top floor of our school building. But my excitement quickly faded after a less than warm welcome from the 5th-grade students. Not only did the 5th-grade girls tease me, the girls in my 3rd-grade class didn't like the idea either. Sure, my parents and teachers lavished accolades and praise. But from the other kids, especially those who weren't doing so well, there was quite a bit of backlash about my studious behavior and zealous attitude towards learning and reading.

When my family moved to a different South Philadelphia neighborhood at the start of 4th grade, I saw my chance to start over – to be labeled as something other than the smart kid. I purposely didn't want to win because I was afraid of what other folks would think of me and how they would respond to me. Sound familiar?

At my new school, I was ahead of most students, too. My teachers loved that I was bright and smart. My classmates did not. This time it was two sisters, Sonya and Gina, who had problems with me "showing off." Sonya, who was in my class, threatened that if I raised my hand, she was going to get Gina, a fifth grader that had been held back a year, to beat me up.

Being smart meant being called a show-off and losing friends.

I needed a different plan. My brilliant strategy: I will not be the first one to turn in my work. The teacher would hand out worksheets and I'd usually finish first. But I developed the habit of pretending I was still working so I wouldn't have to be the first to walk my work to the teacher's desk. Problem solved, right? Sure. Then the teacher had to go and change things.

We'd been given a worksheet to complete in math class. I was the first one finished. When I looked up and saw that everyone else was still working, instead of raising my hand to let the teacher know I was finished I sat there and waited. I didn't want to be first. While I pretended to work on my paper, another girl raised her hand to signal that she was finished. The teacher called her to her desk, looked over her paper, and then gave her a prize.

That was the beginning of my love/hate relationship with owning my brilliance. On one hand, I wanted to be the first one finished and win the prize. On the other hand, I didn't want to be ostracized or attacked. So I lied to myself: Prizes were stupid. I didn't really want them. Being excited about winning was showing off, and I didn't want to be a show-off. In fact, girls that did "show off" by being smart and answering questions were snobs. I didn't want to be a snob. I wanted people to like me.

It was years before I broke free from feeling embarrassed about being smart or feeling ashamed for wanting to be seen. I missed so many opportunities because I refused to be honest about what I wanted. I wanted to run for student council in 9th grade, but I was afraid that people would be mad at me for "showing off." Throughout high school and my early college years, I let opportunities pass by because I didn't want to be singled out.

Deep down, I really wanted to be the girl who boldly raised her hand to answer first, the girl who gladly welcomed opportunities to lead. But I had lied to myself for so long that I didn't know how to break out of the shell I had created. I both admired and resented other girls who were comfortable and confident in the spotlight.

I struggled with this until my third year in college when I was fortunate enough to find a few amazing mentors. These women helped me break through the eclipse blocking my desire to lead and be in the spotlight. I held leadership positions on Drexel's gospel choir, the Campus Activities Board, Disciples InDeed (an on-campus Bible Study Group), and I was a worship leader in Drexel's Christian Fellowship. I was a Resident Assistant and Orientation Leader for new students. I even competed for and earned a place as an Orientation Supervisor.

Are You Trying to Talk Yourself into What You Don't Want?

"To believe in something, and not to live it, is dishonest." — Mahatma Gandhi

One of the techniques we learn as coaches is to help clients shift their perspective or reframe their situation. If you reframe how you see things, you can change your inner and outer dialogue. Once those two changes are made, you can take action from a place of power rather than react from a place of fear or frustration.

I remember the dread and drain of feeling trapped in a job I hated. It was a "good job," but it wasn't fulfilling. I knew I was capable of more – doing more, earning more, and having more impact. Not only that, but I didn't trust or respect the people I was working for and with. A normal shift or reframing that a coach would suggest is to focus on being grateful for having a job. But there was another shift I needed to make: It is okay to outgrow where you are.

My heart started racing. I felt dizzy, weak, and had a hard time concentrating. An overwhelming sadness folded around me like a swaddling cloth. I felt constrained by it on every side. It was Sunday night, and this was my body's response to the coming dread of tomorrow – another Monday morning. If you have ever been in the grip of an anxiety attack, you know how draining it can be – physically and emotionally. Even if you haven't experienced a full-blown panic attack, you do know what it is like to dread Monday morning.

This was the life I lived for years. The panic attacks were the worst when I was a teacher. I taught 5th –grade for two years that felt incredibly long and were extremely stressful. I knew that I wanted to use my gift of teaching to change lives – but the role of an elementary teacher was not the best platform for me. At the end of my second year of teaching, I made the difficult decision that I would not be going back for a third year.

Now, I could have seen the $80,000 education, the hours spent student-teaching and serving in AmeriCorps, and all the preparation for the six-hour exam as a loss. Instead, I focused on what those experiences taught me. I learned about my capacity for compassion and commitment. And I learned how much I truly did want to help other people succeed. One of the most important lessons I learned was this: If you don't like where you are – you have the choice and power to change things.

I could have chosen to wallow in a career that I was clearly ill-suited for. Had I made that decision, I am sure it would have made me a worn and complacent woman, full of regret and self-doubt like so many women I see. They have settled for less than their calling, and having blocked their own brilliance, suffer from perpetual burn-out. But I chose a different journey. Rather than become comfortable with self-pity, I committed to making changes. That commitment has carried me from classroom teacher to award-winning corporate training professional, all the way to making the leap from employee to entrepreneur.

It is always important to be grateful for what you have and where you are. Being grateful allowed me to be present in a job that I didn't like. But acknowledging that I had outgrown my role opened the door for me to freely and confidently look for what was next. My inner dialogue became one of excitement about what was possible. I stopped trying to talk myself into staying in a job that was killing my spirit. And as I began to be honest with others and myself and ask for what I really wanted, the opportunities and support began to show up.

Have You Defined Success in a Way That's Meaningful to You?

There are lots of ways to define success. One way people define it is "to live life on your own terms." To truly love life on your own terms, you have to know what you really want. Too many times we are pushed to go after what we are "supposed" to want, without giving adequate attention to what we actually want. That "supposed" wanting is usually there because of external factors that condition us and influence our thoughts about what's right and what's not, what's a good purpose and what's not, and so on.

Being honest about what you really want is the foundation of meaningful success that's aligned with your purpose and values. When you are unclear or dishonest about what you want, you are likely to spend years:

- Approaching life aimlessly, with no sense of real purpose, or
- Pursuing a path that, on a deep level, you know doesn't belong to you.

In both circumstances, you will find it hard to express your full brilliance. No matter how much you try to sell yourself on a particular goal, it will be difficult to invest in it unless you really want it. Your internal conflict will always find a way to hinder your progress – it's the perfect recipe for self-sabotage.

The good news: when you are honest about what you really want, everything shifts. Not only will you feel a different level of energy, but you will also experience a sense of peace and trust. That's when you are positioned to share your brilliance with the world and enjoy the prosperity you desire: in work, business, life, relationships, and your finances.

Are You Avoiding Making Difficult Decisions?

"You can't make decisions based on fear and the possibility of what might happen." — Michelle Obama

One of the reasons we avoid what we really want is because having it often requires making difficult decisions.

- If you really want to be a full-time entrepreneur, you'll have to decide to leave the security and salary of your job.
- If you want to get married and build a family, you'll have to decide to end a stagnant or unhealthy relationship.
- If you want to stop living in fear, you may have to decide to talk to someone about the abuse you suffered in the past or are currently suffering. Or,
- If you want to break free from the chains of addiction, you have to decide to be honest about your vice of choice – whether it's gambling, sex, overeating, overspending, alcohol, or drugs.

Your chances at breaking through the eclipse blocking your full brilliance are hinged to having the courage to make decisions. Decisions that may cause you short-term discomfort but have long-term benefits. So how do you find the courage to make these decisions?

Before you make any important decision, pray.

Praying allows you to focus on what matters. You relinquish your ego and selfish will so you can embrace higher ambitions that are connected to your purpose and intricately tied to the lives of those you were meant to serve.

Learn to listen to your intuition.

A determining factor in major decisions is not just logical reasoning. There are times when the cons seemingly outweigh the pros, and yet you still hear that small voice telling you to take a step. Faith, intuition, fate, destiny, whatever name you call it, there are times when you just have to trust your vision and move forward.

Carefully seek the advice and support of others.

Sometimes, it can be helpful to seek the advice of people whose lives you admire when making an important decision. There is always an abundance of available opinions, so be careful when choosing whom to listen to. Ultimately, it is up to you to determine your best course of action.

Though many people may be affected by your decisions, you are the only one responsible for your decisions. Turn the pressure of making the right decision into courage to stand up for your vision and what you believe.

Are You Bright or Brilliant? Spend time reflecting on the following questions:

- How are you being dishonest about what you really want?
- When have you felt constrained by someone else's expectations?

- What concessions have you made, personally and professionally, to ensure that someone else was comfortable with your decisions?
- How would your success and contentment level change if you refused to live by other people's expectations?

Step Into Your Purpose: Banish mediocrity and settling for less from your mindset.

Start being honest about what you want. Get it out of your heart and head and tell the world. Write it down, create a vision board, and tell a trusted friend or coach. Watch how your confidence and excitement increases the more you write it, see it, and say it. Learn how to expect and receive other people being excited about what you want and wanting to support you.

From My Heart to Yours...

It's very easy to get lulled into settling for less than what we are capable of being, doing, or having. We find a good job, settle with average performance, and yet seem puzzled when the quality of our life is less than what we want. No amount of prayers can bring you lasting peace and joy when you are not aligned with what you have been called to do.

4 - START ASKING BETTER QUESTIONS

Brilliant Women Know: Complaining and negative self-talk do not serve their purpose. They ask better questions, which lead to better answers, which lead to result-producing actions.

Bright women have a vocabulary that's filled with negative labels and conversations that are full of complaints. They are talkers and disciplined wishers that never make consistent progress towards their goals. They spend so much time labeling themselves as failures, viewing their situation as hopeless, and thinking about all the things that could go wrong, they convince themselves that it's not worth even trying. So they never make consistent effort, and when pressed they have a lengthy list of reasons why they can't, don't, or won't pursue their purpose-based passion.

One of the common excuses people make for not taking action towards pursuing their purpose is money. They look at their financial situation and say, "I don't have the money to…" or they look at their ideas and say, "I'll never get anyone to fund this project." They are making a classic mistake that keeps too many brilliant women from doing the work they have been called to do: they label their situation instead of asking for what they need.

I hear these labels all the time: "I'm broke, I don't have money, I could never afford that, I could never, I can't." Sadly, most people line up their lives according to those labels, creating self-imposed boundaries for their dreams and their lives.

When I made the decision to move to Minnesota in 2009, I was in desperate need of a change. In the two years prior to landing in the Twin Cities, I had relocated to Philadelphia, and faced several challenges in my personal and professional relationships while working full-time and starting my coaching practice part-time.

When my marriage ended in December of 2008, I remember spending days in bed hating every commercial for diamond wedding rings. The four-bedroom house I had purchased had a shallow echo with just my daughter and me in it. The mortgage and household bills were crushing me and it began to feel like I was suffocating. "Stressed" was an understatement to describe how weighted down I felt. I was drowning in a cocktail of emotions: I felt embarrassed, scared, depressed, angry, disappointed, isolated, and confused.

Day and night, my mind raced with questions: Why me? How could I make such stupid decisions? Why don't things ever work out for me? How am I ever going to get my life back to where it was? And then there were the "labels" running through my head: broke, broken, betrayed, stupid, divorced, victim, unwanted, damaged, hurt, pitiful, crushed...any of this feel familiar to you?

I made it through that winter. I survived that spring. By the fall of 2009, I had decided not to wallow in those questions or be defined by those labels. It wasn't easy and it didn't happen overnight. But I kept making new and better decisions, based on better questions:

- What did I really want?
- What did I need in order to get it?
- What did I already have that could help me get where I wanted to be?

- What did I need to let go of?
- Who could and would help me?

Here's what I decided: I wanted to start over. I wanted a better life and environment for my daughter and me. I needed geographic distance from my past bad decisions and the people who judged me based on those decisions. I wanted let go of the emotional and material stuff I had accumulated that wasn't serving my healing. And I wanted space and support to develop into the woman and mother I wanted to be.

My gut told me that I wasn't going to get those things in Philadelphia or Delaware. So I made one of the gutsiest moves of my life: I packed up everything I could afford to move and relocated to St. Paul, Minnesota. I didn't know anyone in Minnesota. I had only been there twice before – once to receive my master's degree from Capella University, and a second time to go look for apartments after I decided to move there.

This wasn't a fly-by-night decision. Prior to moving, I did a ton of research online before I chose Minnesota. After I visited there to scout apartments and neighborhoods, I joined Meetup.com and found a group for single mothers. I asked the members of that group about different neighborhoods and schools. A week after I was here, I attended my first event and met a few of the women that I had talked to online. My daughter and I are still friends with the women from that group and their daughters.

Since moving to Minnesota, I've gotten remarried, been recognized by the women's business community here, and been able to grow my business. My daughter is thriving and happy. I feel truly blessed to have a second family in a place I have come to love, snowy winters and all.

Moving to Minnesota helped me let go of the past and create the space I needed to grow. It was one of the best decisions I made. Had I not asked different questions, I would not have been open to better answers. By refusing to label myself as broke, broken, unwanted, stupid, etc., I was able to grow into exactly who I was called to be, and create the life, relationships, and abundance I wanted.

Are You Making Excuses or Looking for Opportunities?

"I can't cut a check to someone who finds excuses …rather than finds the opportunity" — Mark Cuban

Mark Cuban delivered this brilliant line in an episode of Shark Tank. Shark Tank is a show where entrepreneurs and small business owners pitch their business ideas before a panel of billion-dollar investors. The hope is that contestants will have their business funded by one or more of the investors on the panel.

That line was Mark's response to a contestant who had started giving a list of reasons for why she hadn't positioned her business to be more profitable. I'm sure she thought she was providing rational, logical reasons, but Mr. Cuban was quick to define her words as excuses. Not only that, he took it a step further and decided he had no further interest in her business because she was focused on excuses instead of opportunities.

There are plenty of people with ideas for a business, a book, a non-profit organization, or a project that has the potential to change lives. They might even have a billion-dollar idea. But since all they can see is the work it will take to get from where they are to where they want to be, they never take the steps to turn their idea into reality.

Then there are those who have trained themselves to look beyond the work required and see the payoff for pursuing their purpose-based passion. Because they intentionally look for opportunities rather than obstacles, guess what keeps showing up? More opportunities.

After being in the Twin Cities for just two years, I landed a speaking engagement at a leadership conference of a well-known university here. A colleague of mine was amazed that I'd landed the opportunity, and wanted to know how I got it. Her story: she's been in Minnesota all her life and has always wanted to speak there but didn't have a website, didn't know anybody on the inside, didn't have a one-sheet...she had a few more reasons on her list, too. I'm sure you know people with a similar story and list. According to them, they never seem to get what they want. And the questions they ask you seemed to be coated with a mix of curiosity and jealousy.

The catalyst for the door to open to that speaking opportunity was the networking I had done before I even moved to the Twin Cities. The sister of one of the women in that MeetUp.com group for single moms invited me to talk to the university's leadership advisory team. They invited me to help their larger group with social media, and that opened the door for me to be referred as a speaker for another event, and then another.

When I relocated to Minnesota, I could have let the fact that I knew no one here be an obstacle to growing my business. Instead, I looked for every opportunity to build a solid professional network with women of influence and vision. Each time I let go of my past so I could grasp an opportunity aligned with my vision, another door appeared.

What you look for makes all the difference in what you get. If you are not getting the results you really want, check to see if your actions are in alignment with your intentions.

I admit that sometimes you have to look hard for the opportunities. It can feel like you don't have enough:

- Opportunities
- Time or money
- Support
- Connections
- Luck
- Faith

It can be easy to focus on what's missing in your life. Seeing things you think your success depends on as a velvet rope, keeping you from the red carpet experiences you want. But what if it is you? What if it is you spending more time focused on the steps you think are missing, instead of putting in the work to create what you need?

How many opportunities were missed because you didn't ask for them? How many doors stayed closed because you were waiting for someone to open them for you or give you a key, instead of knocking? Or because you assumed the door was closed because someone else told you it was? More importantly, how long will you keep your gifts and talents hidden from the world because you feel entitled to a lucky break?

The truth: You make and accept excuses instead of asking for what you need because deep down you don't really think you deserve success. If you really believed in your vision, there would be no excuse that could hold you back. As long as the excuses stay floating around in your head, they subconsciously displace the faith and courage required to move forward.

There's always a better question.
If your conversation is full of excuses as to why you can't create the life you really want, I challenge you to ditch the labels and start

asking questions. Instead of saying, "I don't have the money for _____," ask, "How can I find the money for _____?" Instead of saying: "I'm a single mom, I'll never be able to _____," ask, "Who can help me_____?"

Other questions you can ask:

- What can I do to raise capital for _____?
- Where can I get advice?
- Who's done this before?
- What information do I need?
- How can I earn more money?
- How can I reduce my expenses, so I can save more?
- Who can help me think of options I'm not seeing?

Forget About Everyone Else, What Are You Telling Yourself?

Death and life are in the power of the tongue, and those who love it will eat its fruits. — Proverbs 18:21 (NES Translation)

Words have incredible power. We adapt to become whatever we consistently hear about ourselves. What negative messages about yourself do you replay over and over again in your mind? They could be negative words that other people have spoken to you, or they could be discouraging messages you tell yourself.

Years ago as a 5th grade teacher, I studied about the impact of praise and high expectations on performance. When you look at successful teachers, they not only believe in their students' ability to achieve, but they also consistently communicate that expectation. They get that their words have the power to shape and inspire improved performance.

I ask you to stop for a minute and think about the expectations you have for your life. How do you talk to yourself about your dreams and goals? Is your internal dialogue full of praise and encouragement? Are your responses to opportunities, ideas, and experiences that could open doors for you ambiguous and tentative? Disciplined wishers lack the commitment to honestly pursue their purpose. Their internal and external conversations are full of phrases like:

- I was thinking about it.
- I might.
- I'll see.
- Maybe.
- I don't know.
- I'll try.

These responses set an expectation of uncertainty and ambiguity, two enemies of success. If your conversation is filled with ambiguity about how you will perform and what you will do, then expect the same of your results. You might be successful, maybe you'll finally start your business, you'll try to finish that certification, or you'll see if you can save enough money to hire a coach.

Do you expect that you can accomplish your purpose? Do you expect that God has opened every door you need? Do you believe that you have everything you need for "good" success? Then speak like it and live like it.

How Do You Face Closed Doors?

"Knock and the door shall be opened to you." — Matthew 7:7

If the end result of knocking is that the door will be opened, it must have started in a closed state.

Bright women see closed doors as a bad thing. They hang their head in defeat, go into panic mode, or try to manipulate people and situations to get access to what they want. They will even use other people's keys in an attempt to get in. Brilliant women know that we are simply encouraged to knock. You may have to knock more than once. And you may have to wait for a response. Some doors open faster than others, but they do and will open. Here are a few more thoughts on how to K.N.O.C.K. and reap the rewards of your door being opened.

Keep your faith: The faith it takes to knock is the same faith required to keep you standing at the door. When most are ready to walk away because it's taking too long or because other things with immediate benefit are more easily accessible, what will you do? It takes faith to stand and wait, to hold onto a vision no one else can see but you. Keep your faith by tending to it like a gardener cultivating award-winning roses.

Never give in to doubt and fear: It is okay to have doubt and fear. The key is to not allow those feelings to move you from your position. This happens when you try to reason with the doubt and fear, which are only feelings (not truth). A better strategy is to acknowledge what you feel and speak the truth to your doubt and fear until they get smaller and smaller.

Out the ordinary expectations: If you are looking for the door to be opened the ordinary way or only how you think it should happen, you may miss your opportunity. Think of all the ways a door might open. It could open from the bottom like a garage door, spin like a revolving door, or slide open. Or maybe there is a small opening at the bottom that you will have to shrink to fit through. (Maybe losing the ego and attitude will help you fit.)

Choose: We have so much power in our ability to choose. Choose to stand your ground. Choose to be grateful. Choose to forgive. Choose to be genuinely happy for other people. Choose to do what's uncomfortable if it will get you to what's next. When you don't realize your ability to choose, you unconsciously tie your potential to your emotions, which are subject to change. Choosing to respond in faith, regardless of what and how you feel, fuels your ability to live without limits.

Keep your heart and mind guarded: Be careful of what you allow in and whom you allow to sow into you. If you are standing at a door, waiting for it to open, you need your cheerleaders. Surround yourself with those who will patiently wait with you, passing the time with words of encouragement. Read, find inspiring music, watch inspiring movies, do whatever you must to keep your mind and heart prepared for what awaits you on the other side of the door.

Remember, all you need is one door to open at a time. If you are waiting for all the doors to be opened before you pursue your purpose-based passion, you will never get started. Saying that you are waiting for things to "get right" is an excuse. Waiting for things to change, like your finances, your job, your spouse, your kids, your friends, or your situation, implies that there is nothing else you can do. If patience is a virtue, avoidance and procrastination are vices that contradict its value. Don't avoid making decisions or put off doing what you can.

Allowing your vision to be put on hold while you wait for things to work out will only lead to frustration and disappointment. Your life will become stagnant and uninspired. This doesn't mean you throw all caution to the wind and leap without looking. It does mean that you rely on your faith, follow your intuition, and take wise steps towards living your purpose and working your passion. Your situation may not be perfect, but you can perfectly position yourself for the opportunities you need.

If you can see a clear vision for what you want, be determined to find a way to make it happen. Where there's a vision – make a way.

Are You Bright or Brilliant? Spend time reflecting on the following questions:

- What situations are you telling yourself have to be perfect before you can pursue your purpose?
- What labels that you have been using to define your situation do you need to let go of?
- What seemingly closed doors that you have been avoiding do you need to knock on?
- What is your intuition telling you? Is it time to open them now, practice patience, or look for another option?

Step Into Your Purpose: Be conscious of what you say and what you expect.

Start looking for the opportunities you need. And be willing to create them if your intuition prompts you. Make over your conversation by making "I will _____!" your mantra.

- From: "I'm thinking about starting a business" to "I <u>will</u> start my business this year."
- From: "Maybe I'll give them a call" to "I <u>will</u> follow up with those potential clients today."
- From: "I'll try to finish my book" to "I <u>will</u> write every day for 20 minutes until I finish my book."

From My Heart to Yours…

The negative labels that you use to describe yourself and your situation do not serve you or your calling. They keep you imprisoned in a state of hopelessness. I pray that you allow your Creator to give you new words, new questions, and new ways of seeing yourself. Open your heart, eyes, and ears to receive the abundance of love and grace supplied on a daily basis. And ask for what you want with gratitude and confidence that you will be answered.

5 - CHANGE YOUR PERSPECTIVE ON FAILURE

Brilliant Women Know: Failures, missteps, and mistakes are just stepping-stones on their path to purpose.

Bright women avoid failure at all cost. In their minds, failure is synonymous with shame; it's the worst thing that could happen to them. Rather than feel the disappointment of failure, they set low expectations and settle for mediocrity. They live with an inner critic that constantly reminds them of every failure, misstep, and mistake. And they perceive criticism in the looks and tones of the people they encounter. Led by their pride, they forget that every successful person's journey is paved with some failure.

I could fill an entire book with the failures, missteps, and mistakes I've made in my life. In some instances, I didn't know any better. At other times, I knew better but didn't know any other way to get what I wanted. I spent many nights and journal pages crying over the mistakes I'd made, fearing that I was too far-gone to be able to recover.

In 2008, I made one of the biggest mistakes in my life and married a man who was not a good partner for me. Oddly enough, I met him at a time when I was getting everything I wanted in my life. I had a great job that allowed me to work from home full-time. I was launching my career coaching business on the side. I had relocated from New York to Philadelphia so I could be closer to my family. Financially I was set, having restored my credit from bankruptcy years earlier. I had even lost over 80 pounds – I felt good and looked good, too. It finally felt like the love that I wanted was showing up in my life.

In just eight short months, I went from being happily single, to miserably married, to filing for divorce. I did everything I could to try and make my marriage work. After spending hours worrying, crying, and reading everything I could find on Christians and divorce, I finally went to my pastor's wife. It was her words that gave me the courage to leave.

In the midst of making that decision and the outcomes that followed, I felt like a failure. But when I think about it now, leaving that marriage was a lesson I lived that became a stepping-stone for where I am today.

Mistakes – we have all made them. Some of them have been small with minimal impact. Others have been enormously public mistakes seen by many. Then there are the mistakes that no one saw, but that derailed our true course and left us feeling like we would never be restored.

Some people live in the shadow of their past mistakes and failures. They replay every bad decision and every feeling of shame and disappointment attached to the consequences. If fear based on past failures stands in the way of pursuing your purpose, start the healing process by forgiving yourself:

- Accept what's happened and decide to move on.
- Grieve over any loss and give yourself time to heal. Remember, each person's healing process is different.

- Start trusting yourself. As new opportunities come to make better decisions, let go of harshly judging your choices. Being confident in your decisions helps you get free to go after what you really want.
- Stop defining yourself by your fumbles and failures.
- Choose to get back in the game and claim your spot as the MVP in your life.

Are You Afraid of Failure?

"Don't be afraid of failure. Be afraid of living your life by default."
— Tai Goodwin

There is at least one common pattern you will find in the life of every successful person. Regardless of how much money they have now, where they started or even how they became successful, they failed. Then they picked themselves up and tried again. In most cases that's over-simplifying it. In most cases, it looks more like: fail, fail, almost got it, nope, missed it, totally blew it, and finally got it! And depending on whom we are talking about, there might be a few more fails and misses before they finally "got it."

Want proof? Consider the path of these success stories:

- **Oprah Winfrey:** Endured numerous career setbacks including being fired from her job as a television reporter because she was "unfit for TV."
- **J. K. Rowling:** Was depressed, divorced, and raising a child on welfare as a single parent while attending school and writing her novel.
- **Vera Wang:** Failed to make the U.S. Olympic figure-skating team before being passed over at Vogue for the editor-in-chief position.

- **John Grisham:** Faced rejection by 16 agents and 12 publishing houses.
- **Michael Jordan:** Was cut from his high school basketball team.
- **Sidney Poitier:** After his first audition was told by the casting director, "Why don't you stop wasting people's time and go out and become a dishwasher or something?"
- **Steven Spielberg:** Was turned down by the USC's School of Theater, Film and Television three times.
- **R. H. Macy (Macy's):** Started seven businesses that failed before finally getting it right with his flagship store in New York City.
- **Soichiro Honda:** Was turned down by Toyota Motor Corporation after interviewing for a job as an engineer.

Here's an interesting observation: Early on we are praised for everything. We take a step – Yay! We signal for the potty – Hurray! We color inside the lines – Fantastic! We recite the alphabet – Amazing! Then we get to school and things change. We become aware of what we don't know, can't do, what we are weak in, not good at, etc. And so starts the internal list we keep of where we fall short, and then all we can see is how we don't measure up to others.

So many bright women never unleash their brilliance because they keep referring to their list of failures as if it is a dictionary that defines them. Every time an opportunity comes up they go back to their dictionary and find a reason why they will fail. They forget there is another list: the one with their wins, successes, and triumphs. It's the list that shows what you did after you have gotten up from the fall. This is the most valuable list.

Do You Really Want to Be Successful?

The thin line that separates those who reach their goals and those who are less successful is action. How much do you really want to pursue your purpose? And then the most important question: What are you going to do about it?

Are you willing to make the sacrifices, acquire the discipline, and experience the discomfort of stretching beyond where you are today? What if going after what you want means stepping away from the traditional road and daring to walk alone to blaze your own trail? Are you still willing to pursue your passion and purpose against the grain of the economy, naysayers, unappreciative bosses, friends that don't understand, judgmental spectators, and even your own inner critic?

Think of success like a garden: your potential is the seed and requires good soil (or purpose) to grow. Till the ground with desire, root out the weeds, and then you will be prepared for your success to bloom.

In another Shark Tank episode, I heard Daymond John (billionaire founder of FUBU and branding expert) say something incredible! He said that it took him nine years to earn a profit in his first business – nine years! He was responding to a contestant who wanted funding from the Sharks (investors) so he could have a salary while launching his business. The contestant brings to mind people who want a profitable business tomorrow, or who want a six-figure job next week. John's words confirmed what I believe: There is no overnight success; there is just every-day perseverance.

How long are you willing to pursue your purpose? One year? Three years? Nine years? There are people who put everything on the line: they sleep in their cars, mortgage their houses, cash in their 401Ks and borrow hundreds of thousands of dollars from friends and family in order to pursue their purpose-based passion. Some of them succeed, some of them fail, and sadly some of them quit. How long will you work to see your vision come to pass? If you need to be "successful" or make $10,000 in the next month or else you are calling it quits, then quit today. If it's not worth the wait, don't bother investing anything at all.

Before you quit or determine that things aren't happening fast enough, remember that real purpose is not just about you. Your quitting too soon will have an impact on all the people waiting for the brilliance you are meant to bring into the world. As a corporate game changer, a visionary entrepreneur, a master storyteller, or an author – no matter what your gift, the world is waiting for you.

We are really good at encouraging others to live their dreams. We enthusiastically encourage our children, our spouse or partner, other family members, our co-workers, our colleagues, and members of our church and community. Remember that your purpose is important, too. Too important to let negative self-talk about past failures hold you back.

You deserve success because you are here. If you are here, you have a purpose. It's up to you to discover, pursue, and enjoy the purpose you were created for.

One of the tapes that used to constantly play in my head was, "Who do you think you are?" Every time I wanted to make a decision or step into uncharted territory, my inner gremlins would begin whispering in my ear. I was able to dismiss those negative messages by reminding myself of who I am and what I have been called to do. I remind myself that success has been written into my destiny – whether I believe I deserve it or not.

Do you have a hard time believing that you were purposed to succeed? Let me give you 101 reasons you deserve success:

- Reason #1: You have been given life.
- Reason #2-101: See Reason #1.

The very fact that space has been made for you and that breath has been granted to you entitles you to all the success you are willing to work for. If you are not finding the success you want, it is not because you don't deserve it. It's because there's an internal conflict blocking you from being honest about what you really want.

The work that leads to success is an inside job. It begins with your belief system and the intentions you set. Do you believe you deserve to be successful? Or are you running a checklist in your head of all the things you think you must do to deserve success. Believing you deserve success is different from actually having success. The "having" comes from taking the right actions. But here's the catch – you will never be fully motivated to take the right actions if you don't think you deserve success in the first place.

If you've put your purpose on the back burner because you are afraid of failing, it's time to encourage yourself. As you start seeing your past failures as lessons you have lived, the next steps to take become clearer, the opportunities you need show up, and suddenly you find you have everything you need to pursue your purpose.

Are You Comparing or Celebrating?

"Stop comparing your insides with someone else's outside." — Hugh MacLeod

This simple line is a gem. It's something every one of us brave enough to take the journey toward fulfilling our purpose needs to digest. It needs to take root in our hearts, minds and souls.

Comparing our journey and development to what we see of other people only leads to jealousy and resentment. Both are detriments to true prosperity. Comparing yourself to someone who is in a season of harvest while you are still sowing the seeds of your success will create doubt, insecurity, and fear. None of those emotions can help you. In fact, they chip away at the faith that fuels your action. The more your faith diminishes, the easier it becomes to step away from your purpose and settle for mediocrity.

Instead of comparing yourself (that includes your journey, your progress, and your results), look for what you can learn from someone else's success. Explore their story for insights, questions, and truths that you can apply to your journey. Learn from their experience; don't yearn for their life. Remember, you are not seeing everything they had to go through, and probably grow through, to get to where they are now. There is no such thing as overnight success for anyone.

Case in point: The 2013 U.S. pop culture sensation Psy, a rapper from South Korea. The video for his song, "Gangnam Style," holds the Guinness World Record as the most liked video in YouTube's history. Psy is also the very first South Korean artist to top the charts on iTunes. The video first started going viral back in July of 2012, but guess how long he's been an entertainer? 10 years! That's how long it took him to build a following in South Korea. While he may seem like an overnight success to us, he's been at it for 10 YEARS.

Maybe you planned to finish your degree by now. Or maybe you dreamed that by now you would be your own boss. Or maybe you just knew you were going be debt-free, ready to retire, and planning the ultimate mission trip. While you can see so clearly what you want, the actual manifestation of your vision may take some time. Depending on the scale of your vision, it may take lots of time. If you find yourself dissatisfied with where you are, remember that one small step is all that's needed to make progress.

No matter how small a step you take, forward movement is all that's required for you to make progress. You may not have gotten as much done as you wanted, or be as far along as you planned, but rest assured you are exactly where you are supposed to be.

Progress, like success, is gradual. Trust that the small changes you make over time are gradually helping you move closer to your goals. Instead of despising small beginnings, accept, acknowledge, and appreciate each small step. When you find yourself feeling discouraged, reach out to your support system to help you stay the course.

Are You Bright or Brilliant? Spend time reflecting on the following questions:

- How is fear of failure showing up in your life?
- What negative messages are on your internal tape recorder?
- What missteps and mistakes do you need to forgive yourself for?
- How would your confidence change if you stopped comparing yourself to others and started celebrating your successes?

Step Into Your Purpose: Release your fear of failure.

Get out your pen (or laptop). It's time to do some writing:

- Write a letter of forgiveness to yourself.
- Then write a letter to someone whose journey you admire – express your genuine happiness about their success.
- Finally, write a letter to someone who needs encouragement.

From My Heart to Yours…

Just because other people have quit or failed, that doesn't mean that's your destiny, too. What if your journey is meant to inspire others? What if your struggle is tied to God's plan for someone else's victory? What if your light is meant to be a beacon for people who haven't even been born yet? Failing doesn't make you worthless – failing adds value by way of authentic experiences that you can share with others. Fumbles are not fatal. I pray that you learn to see failure as an ally in helping you create a purposeful path. The sooner you change your perspective on failure, the sooner you can start looking for the lessons you have lived from those experiences.

6 - GIVE YOURSELF PERMISSION TO SOAR

Brilliant Women Know: They will never win trying to run someone else's race.

Bright women are constantly comparing themselves to other people. And they make decisions about their journey based on other people's expectations and comfort. They have learned to be internal contortionists – twisting their wants and needs to try and fit in. They waste their time and life trying to follow popular paths. They fail to realize they were never created to fit in. The very light and brilliance they admire in others, they fail to cherish in themselves. They remain lost and confused until they finally realize they are using the wrong map and trying to run someone else's race.

Earlier I shared the story about a conversation with my high school counselor that drove me away from pursuing my passion. Unfortunately, Mrs. Kelsey, my misguided guidance counselor, would be just one of the people in my life with lowered or different expectations than I had for myself. In fact, almost every major decision I've made has been challenged and questioned, sometimes by those closest to me:

- When I told my mother I wanted to major in fashion design, she immediately set up a meeting with our pastor to talk me out of it.

- A close family member thought I was snobby because I wanted to live on campus instead of staying at home while in college.
- A close work colleague was angry when I decided to leave Baltimore and go to New York for my dream job as Training Specialist at Barnes & Noble.
- Family members frowned on my decision to move to Minnesota.
- When I decided that I was going to leave my six-figure job to be a full-time coach and speaker, a few people close to me shook their heads in disbelief, telling me I was being ungrateful.

One of the hardest things to do is stick to decisions that put you in opposition of the people that you most crave acceptance from. At the time, choosing to follow my own path was painful. But I know that if I had based my decision on their insight into my future, I would have never moved forward in my life, career, or business. The pain and loneliness I endured is nothing compared to the eclipse of living my life based on other people's fears or self-imposed constraints.

Lesson lived: Never doubt your purpose because someone else can't see it.

To reclaim your brilliance, you will have to be prepared to give yourself permission to soar. You'll have to believe in your purpose and vision, even if you are the only one who can see it clearly. There will be people who genuinely don't get you. Then there will be those who get you, see your potential, and want to harness your light for themselves. There will even be people who want to dim your light so they can have company in their darkness. Then there are those brilliant souls who generously sow into your life with their light. Find one of those people. Be one of those lights for someone else.

Are You Allowing Other People's Expectations to Determine Your Path?

I heard Wayne Dyer say, "Never let other people's idea about what is possible or impossible for you take up space in your imagination." Here's a question I have for you: What's <u>your idea</u> about what's possible or impossible for you?

It's the teacher in me that believes people will rise to the level of expectation you have for them. High expectation supported by real praise and constructive feedback is the practice of an effective teacher. Unfortunately, most of the teachers we are exposed to, they make mediocrity the standard expectation. Their tendency is to expect people to settle rather than excel. So when you come along, rocking the boat by deciding you want more, you may be hard pressed to find those who will give you genuine praise and feedback. The good news is you can always add people to your network who have the same drive as you and believe in your ability to succeed. Your goal is to intentionally seek those people out.

Even with a supportive network, reaching your goals will be an uphill battle if you don't have high expectations for yourself. So the question is: What do you want for you?

- Do you expect to make an impact in the world?
- Do you expect to live and serve from a place of abundance?
- Do you expect you'll be able to find the resources and people you need?
- Do you expect that you can and will turn your vision into reality?

Realize that yours is the only permission you need to move from being on the verge of success to thriving in your purpose. Why limit yourself to the chicken coop or the lake with other swans when you could be soaring like the eagle you are?

What Are You Waiting For?

"Twenty years from now you will be more disappointed by the things that you didn't do than by the ones you did do. So throw off the bowlines. Sail away from the safe harbor. Catch the trade winds in your sails. Explore. Dream. Discover" — Mark Twain

There are times when it makes perfect sense to wait. Maybe you need more information. Maybe your true intuition, not fear, is whispering, "Not yet." Then there are times when your reasons are just excuses. They might sound like legitimate, logical reasons for not taking action, but if you are honest they are really just self-made boundaries that you've created to keep from failure and disappointment.

Are you ready to stop faking yourself out and lose the wait that has been keeping you grounded? Here's a list of 19 things you don't have to wait for to pursue your purpose and create the life you really want.

Don't wait:

1. For the opportunities you want. Create them.
2. To be asked for what you want or need.
3. For people to like or approve of your idea.
4. To make and take time for yourself and your passion.
5. For your skills to be perfect. You can always learn as you go.
6. For people to reach out to you to start building your network.
7. Until you think you know how everything is going to work out.
8. To finish your degree or complete your professional certifications.
9. To be recognized. Find a way to shamelessly self-promote your wins.
10. To ask for help. Reach out and reach up to create the support you need.

11. For someone to ask you to participate. Show up, join in, and make an impact.
12. For someone else whom you think is "smarter" or "better" to solve the problem first.
13. For someone to appoint you to a leadership role. Find a way to lead without a title.
14. Until you feel like doing something. Your feelings will line up once you take the necessary actions.
15. For someone to give you permission to dream big and create a plan for making your dreams come true.
16. Until you have more experience. Look for opportunities that will allow you to stretch.
17. To disengage from unproductive relationships and conversations that make you doubt your purpose, talents, or vision.
18. To boldly pursue your purpose-based passion without shame, regret, or fear.
19. Until you have all the money you think you need. The resources will find you once you take action.

Speaking of money…Women who settle for mediocrity falsely believe they will never get ahead because they don't have enough money. Their faulty thinking about money, and the resources required to make things happen, stand in the way of pursuing their passion. I've been there, constrained by a mindset that kept me focused on financial survival rather than generating wealth. Are you stuck in that space?

Many women think it is impossible for them to make a six-figure income doing something they love. Or people dream of taking control of their earning potential by working for themselves. In either case, it's rarely money that keeps them from taking action; it's their own limiting beliefs about their possibilities. They wind up settling for whatever they think they can make. Or if they are in business, they settle for whatever they think people will pay them. Refusing to see beyond their own barriers, they settle for being disciplined wishers instead of rewarded risk takers. The reality is, you can make whatever amount of money you want. The only one stopping you is you. Don't believe me? Just ask the thousands of people who have found a way to pursue their passion and earn a sustainable income doing what they love – even during a recession.

It's all about the mindset you choose: If you truly believe you will be successful, you find a way to make it happen. But if deep down you believe you can't, you will never get the success you crave. Instead of focusing on all the reasons you think you can't, think about what is within your reach to make happen. Disciplined wishers constantly complain about what isn't happening for them and how much they will never have. Yet they continue to do the same things day after day after day, believing they have no power to change their situation.

Brilliant women lit by the fire of their purpose-based passion believe there is always a way to find what they need. They are resourceful, resilient, and tenacious when it comes to pursuing their passion. Instead of focusing on what they don't have and labeling their situation, they ask better questions.

Is money the obstacle keeping you from pursuing your passion? Make a decision today that money will not stop you. Start asking better questions and expecting the answers to show up. How can you:

- Find a way to attend that top conference in your industry?
- Rebrand and reposition yourself as a leader in your organization?
- Barter with someone to get your website built, professional headshots taken, or the legal advice you need for your non-profit?

- Get more visibility for your business by leveraging your online and offline network?
- Find investors to sow into your project so you can take your vision to the next level?

Are You Drowning in Doubt or Flying in Faith?

"If you limit your choices only to what seems possible or reasonable, you disconnect yourself from what you truly want, and all that is left is a compromise." — Robert Fritz

Do you struggle with self-doubt, always questioning your purpose? The worst thing about self-doubt is that your fears often become self-fulfilling prophecies. The key to erasing self-doubt is to take action. Each step you take towards living your purpose increases your self-confidence and sharpens your decision-making skills. To silence your inner critic so you can be ready to receive the opportunities awaiting you:

- Identify what's triggering your self-doubt. Are you feeling overwhelmed? Are you comparing yourself to someone else? Are you experiencing the discomfort of trying something new? Tuning in to the source of the insecurity empowers you to address it.
- Stop focusing on past mistakes. You may be subconsciously replaying negative thoughts about past failures and rejection, which prevent you from moving forward. Thoughts like "I can't do this" and "I'm not good enough" become excuses to hide from new experiences and opportunities.

We all make mistakes. Making mistakes doesn't make you a bad or incompetent person – it simply makes you human. Beating yourself up over something you feel you did wrong only leads to a damaging cycle of frustration and procrastination. Consider that life's challenges are an opportunity to learn and grow as a person. Make a decision to accept that while you're not perfect, you are someone who strives to do the best job possible.

The next time you have a self-doubting thought, take a few moments to determine whether it's really true. If your insecurities are getting the better of you, remember that while your past may influence your purpose, it does not determine your destiny. As soon as you catch negative thoughts clouding your vision, replace the defeating messages with positive self-talk. Make the switch each and every time your inner critic shows up.

Are You Bright or Brilliant? Spend time reflecting on the following questions:

- How has self-doubt been keeping you from your purpose?
- What do you need to stop settling for?
- What do you need to give yourself permission to have, be, or do?
- To whom have you been giving permission to sow negative seeds into you or limit the vision you have?

Step Into Your Purpose: Give yourself permission to soar.

Write yourself a letter, granting permission to have the biggest, boldest, most brilliant vision you can think of. And give yourself permission to pursue it with everything that's in you.

I agree with my Creator that I have been designed to _____. I, _____, give myself permission to be: _____. I can and will _____.
Starting this moment, I will pursue my purpose-based passion so I can live in integrity and fulfill my calling.

Write this or type it and post it where you can see it. Share it with the cheerleaders in your network!

From My Heart to Yours...

Rather than sitting back and hoping that an opportunity to pursue your purpose-driven passion will fall into your lap, choose to put your whole heart into going after what you want. Don't quit! Don't settle. The world is waiting for you. If God lives inside you and you are listening, and your heart's motivation is sincere, trust that your thoughts and choices are in line with your Creator.

7 - CONNECT AND COLLABORATE WITH BRILLIANT WOMEN

Brilliant Women Know: We are stronger together. They use their brilliance to light the way for others and seek out the light in other people.

Bright women fight against their own brilliance and work to block the light of other women. There is an underlying theme of fear and jealousy in their life because they sow condescendence and criticism into the lives of others. Putting other women down, creating confusion and discord with their words, and being unwilling to invest in other people are indicators of spiritual immaturity and fear of their own brilliance. They also never invest in themselves – they'd rather look for what is free and easy than discipline themselves to do the work required to live their purpose. Instead of spending their time building bridges, they put up walls.

Is Your Network Working For You or Against You?
There was a time when I didn't have a good network. Like many women, I clung to the relationships I did have even though they were hurting me and not helping me. It's one of the reasons it took me two years to start LaunchWhileWorking.com. Why? Because a woman in my network, whom I considered a trusted advisor, didn't think it was a good idea. She didn't like the name "employedpreneur" (a term I coined for full-time employees with part-time businesses),

and didn't think it was a good concept. So I filed the thought away and kept on working as a career coach. At least I tried to. The idea for helping people who were, like me, launching a business while working full-time was something I just couldn't shake.

In 2011, I launched the site and started a Facebook Group for employedpreneurs. I also started a Blog Talk Radio show – Launch Talk. At its height, Launch Talk was getting over 6,500 downloads a month. In 2012, my work with Launch While Working led to an Honorable Mention as a Small Business Influencer. In 2013, I won the Small Business Influencer Top 100 Champion Award. Imagine my shock when the woman that told me she didn't like the name later advised me that I should use "Employedpreneur" more in my branding, and said how great my idea was, as if we had never talked about it before.

That relationship showed me that I needed different women in my circle. So I set an intention to be connected to powerful women who were living with passion and purpose. I am amazed now when I look at the brilliant women I am connected to – women who generously sow into my life and so brilliantly show up in the world to make an impact in the lives of others. These connections are not a coincidence. I deliberately identified the women I wanted in my network, and started reading everything I could about how to create a powerful professional network.

I found plenty of articles on where to find people, how and when to connect to them, and even what to say to attract them. What I didn't find was a list of the types of people I needed to have in my network. So I created a list that focused on the quality of your connection rather than just how many people you are connected to.

A strong professional network has at least one of the following types of brilliant women and men:

The Mentor: This is the person who has reached the level of success you aspire to have. You can learn from their success as well as their mistakes. Heed their wisdom and experience. Many mentoring relationships last over a period of years, with different peaks of interaction and communication. Mentors offer a unique perspective because they have known you through several peaks and valleys in your life and watched you evolve.

The Coach: The coach is someone who comes in at different times in your life. They help with critical decisions and transitions, and offer an objective view with no strings attached. These relationships are short-term, with different situations requiring a different coach to help you clarify, create, and evaluate a targeted plan of action. They also hold you accountable for the goals you have set for yourself.

The Industry Insider: This is someone in your field who has expert-level information or access to it. This person will keep you educated and in the know of what's happening now and what the next big thing is. Learn from them and invite them to be a sounding board for your next innovative idea or concept.

The Trendsetter: This is someone outside of your chosen industry or niche who always has the latest buzz. It can be on any topic that you find interesting or that has been labeled "hot." The goal in having this person in your network is to look for those connections that spark innovation via the unconventional. It will also help keep you and your conversations interesting.

The Connector: This is a person who has access to people, resources, and information. As soon as they come across something related to you, they are sending you an email or picking up the phone. Your Connector is the person in your circle that constantly gets and answers the question, "Do you know anyone who…?" Connectors are great at uncovering unique ways to make connections, and finding resources and opportunities that most people would overlook.

The Idealist: This is the person in your network whom you can dream with. No matter how "out there" your latest idea is, this is the person who will help you brainstorm ways to make it happen, even if your plans seem totally unrealistic right now. We all need that person who will help us think of potential "how's" without judging our ideas.

The Realist: True to their name, the Realist will help you keep it real. This is the brave soul who will lovingly give you the raised eyebrow when your expectations exceed your effort. These are not people who knock down your dreams. They do challenge you to actively make your dreams happen, though. The realist in your life will lovingly ask how you plan to get promoted when you show up late to every meeting. Or graciously point out how saying that you want to build your bank account conflicts with maxing out your credit cards for a 5-day trip to Jamaica.

The Visionary: Visionaries inspire you by the journey that they are on. They are similar to the Idealist, but the visionary can help you see how to make your dream a reality because they have manifested their own dreams. One personal encounter with this type of person can powerfully change the direction of your thinking and your life. These are the people whose columns, blogs, and books we read. Or whom we sit with in a coffee shop for hours, listening and learning from their lives.

The Partner: You need to have someone who is in a similar place and on a similar path to share your journey with. In this relationship, there is a shared intention of success through sharing. This is a person you can share the wins and woes with. Partners also generously share resources, opportunities, and information. With a true partner there is no competition, jealousy, or envy.

The Wanna-Be: This is someone you can serve as a mentor to. Someone you can sow into and guide based on your experiences and lessons lived. One of the best motivators for pushing through obstacles and hardships is knowing that someone is watching your journey. Consider how many people start to straighten their lives out once they realize they are setting an example for their children.

Whether you are an employee, an employedpreneur, or an entrepreneur, having a strong support system is critical to pursuing your purpose and manifesting your vision. Obviously, you will want to have more than ten people in your network. The trick is to make sure that you are building a diverse network by adding people from different industries, backgrounds, age groups, ethnic groups, etc., who fit into the roles listed above. Building a network by only including people from your current niche, work, religion, or hobbies leaves so many stones unturned and limits your potential opportunities.

Are You Cat Woman or Wonder Woman?

Cat Woman, a popular nemesis of Batman, is portrayed as seductive, cunning, and smart. Her attraction belies her true intent: she's a thief. She works alone, trusts no one, and is always on the prowl for the next victim she can take from. Her weapon is a whip; perfect for beating down her opponents so she can get what she wants.

Wonder Woman, on the other hand, is a truth-seeker who solves problems and restores people and situations. She works for justice and peace. Her true identity is an Amazon princess. Bottom line: she's a warrior with a tiara and a Lasso of Truth. And she gets to her destinations by an invisible jet (sounds like soaring by faith to me).

Wonder Woman also understands the power of collaboration: she hangs with a brilliant crew, the Super Friends, and she's also part of the Justice League.

Cat Women are Brilliance Blockers. Wonder Women are Brilliance Catalysts. As you think about your life and how you connect with other women, ask yourself: Are you a blocker or a catalyst?

I used to run into more Cat Women than Wonder Women. If that's your experience right now, you should know that you attract what you are. Are you throwing shade and criticizing other women, feeling envious of their success? Then you will attract other women of the same ilk. And before you dismiss the lines above and turn the page, let's examine what it really looks like when you are putting up walls instead of leading with your light.

Cat Women are Brilliance Blockers who:
- Look for ways to get, which avoid them having to give.
- Attribute other women's success to luck, lust, or lying.
- Only help when there's something in it for them.
- Give false opinions based on their own insecurities when people ask for feedback.
- Share negative stories and rumors about other women.
- Take advantage of other people's willingness to help.
- Scheme and manipulate to get what they want, instead of asking.
- Sow doubt and disapproval disguised as questions and "constructive criticism."
- Feel justified when they hear or learn of other women failing or struggling.
- Build relationships with other women based on their dislike for someone else.

- Withhold ideas and information out of fear that someone will get ahead faster than they will.
- Have great excuses for why they don't follow through on promises to themselves and other women.
- Intentionally keep other women down so they can appear "better than" and feel superior.

Wonder Women are Brilliance Catalyst who:
- Nurture a spirit of true generosity.
- Celebrate the success of other women.
- Help someone without always needing something in return.
- Give honest feedback and answers that allow people to make informed decisions.
- Share positive reports about other women and refuse to engage in gossip that degrades another person.
- Accept help when they need it from other women with gratitude and humility.
- Ask for what they want and need, from a place of integrity and honesty.
- Sow encouragement and support when other women share their dreams, visions, and goals.
- Pray for women whom they hear are having a hard time, and offer them support.
- Build relationships with other women who are pursuing their purpose-based passion.
- Share ideas and information freely to help light the way for others.
- Hold themselves accountable for doing what they say they are going to do.
- Intentionally look for ways to take other women with them as they soar into greatness.

How Are You Guarding Your Heart?

"Above all else, guard your heart, for it is the wellspring of life." — Proverbs 4:23

It takes guts and sacrifice to pursue your purpose-based passion. Whether you are starting a business, a book, or an amazing project, choosing to start is a road less traveled. So many people give up on their vision, shelving their talents and potential because it feels too hard. They become disheartened when they realize their purpose requires more investment than they are willing to make.

Unfortunately, some of the people in our lives have not only given up on their vision, they want to steer you towards giving up on yours. Some mean well, fearing you will be disappointed if things don't work out. Others are just being downright selfish. They are looking at what the investment in your vision will cost them: less time with you, less money from you, less focus on their problems and drama. Then there are others who are just plainly jealous that you have the audacity to pursue your passion instead of settling for mediocrity and dissatisfaction.

I've run into many of those people in my life. I have had to spend many years removing the message, "Who do you think you are?" that played as background noise at every step I took into a new area, at every reach towards something desired but unfamiliar. To break free from that message that kept me shackled to fear and self-doubt, I had to learn to do two things:

1. Speak back, declaring exactly who I was, and
2. Guard my heart.

Guard your heart like a treasure. And carefully guard your vision by limiting the time you spend around people who consistently choose a negative outlook. If you can't limit the time you spend around them, find a way to put them on "mute."

Be careful whom you ask for feedback and input – all answers are not created equal. As a woman with a purpose, you can't listen to everyone. Be discerning in the conversations you engage in and the answers you allow to seep into your heart, mind, and soul. Trust your intuition about whom to listen to and whom you allow to sow into your life.

Throughout our lives, we meet many different people. Sometimes our work leads us to meet people that we eventually develop personal relationships with. Occasionally, we make new acquaintances through family or friends. Then there are business relationships sparked through networking events. No matter how they begin, the typical nature of relationships is that they grow, and in some cases they end.

Even when there are valid reasons for ending a relationship, terminating those connections can still cause a sense of loss. Though it may be difficult to end things, it's important to understand your life will be better once you end any relationship that drains your energy and threatens your purpose. Be prepared for the disappointment you may feel at having to cut your ties to certain people. And know that any pain you experience is a stepping-stone getting you closer to your purpose.

As much as you value your relationships, there are times you will be compelled to end them. One of those times is when progress towards your purpose and passion is stalled because of the other person. They subtly or even blatantly sabotage your efforts, put down your ideas, or withhold information. Bottom line is that they don't truly have your best interest at heart, unless it benefits them in some way.

Here's a relationship litmus test: If you feel hurt, anxious, and disappointed more often than you feel energized, supported, and appreciated, it may be time to pause the relationship. Today, be confident that if you need to, you can end relationships that constrain you or drain your soul and threaten your purpose.

Are You Bright or Brilliant? Spend time reflecting on the following questions:

- Are the women you are connected to brilliance blockers or brilliance catalysts?
- What negative relationships and attitudes do you need to let go of to attract more brilliance into your life?
- How are you intentionally investing in yourself and sowing into other people?

Step Into Your Purpose: Upgrade your network.

Make a list of the people in your current network. Say a prayer of thanks and send a note of gratitude to the women in your network who have graciously sowed into you and your vision. Set an intention to add healthy relationships with the exact type of women you'd like in your life. Release any relationships that drain your energy and conflict with your spirit.

From My Heart to Yours...

Together we are stronger. I pray that you learn to discern who has your best interest at heart and let go of those who are weighing you down. The level of your enthusiasm and the rate at which you make progress in your purpose are directly related to the support system you have. You are not meant to do everything alone. Pray and ask God to send the people you need and get ready for your divine connections to show up.

PART II
FUEL FOR YOUR JOURNEY

1 - UNMASK YOUR EXCUSES

An excuse is an explanation of a fault given with the intent of being understood and avoiding judgment. Don't be fooled into letting excuses masquerade as reasons why you shouldn't take the next step in pursuing your purpose.

Find yourself making excuses? Trying to explain your lack of interest or motivation as if you are at fault? Dig deeper and take a look at your true desires. Are you really willing to take the next step on the path laid out before you? That unwillingness you feel may be an indicator that you are about to step into something that's not truly meant for you. A sign that you are about to walk a road that leads you away from the core of your purpose. And don't confuse unwillingness with fear. A willing heart is subject to fear no matter how willing it is, and requires commitment and courage to move forward despite the fearful feelings.

Publicly, your excuses masquerade as logical, practical reasons for why you cannot move. Privately, those same excuses become stones that weigh down your spirit. There is freedom in just acknowledging the truth: The excuses come because you don't really want to do something. Whether you are afraid, uninterested, or simply unwilling – the truth is you just don't want to do what you are making an excuse for.

Admitting that you don't want to do something doesn't make you a bad person. And it doesn't make you a failure or a slacker. You are just honestly acknowledging a truth about yourself. Telling the truth will liberate you and is more powerful than any excuse you can come up with. Making excuses will only add guilt and a sense of disappointment to your load. Eventually, you will find yourself paralyzed, unable to make any decision without a sense of anxiety or overwhelming pressure. It's why the simplest questions can spark anger or panic.

Unless you get to the heart of why you are unwilling and address those issues, the excuses will keep coming. It is 100% possible that you are unwilling for all the wrong reasons. You will never know if you avoid getting to the root of the matter. Unmask the excuses, admit you are unwilling, and then deal with the unwillingness head on.

2 - TAKE THE RISKS THAT BRING REWARD

You want the opportunity to pursue your passion and prosper, the freedom to live the lifestyle you want, and success on your own terms? The foundation to having all of those things is integrity: aligning your outside with the purpose and passion that lives on the inside of you. In order to live from a place of integrity, you have to be willing to take risks. I'm not referring to undisciplined, reckless types of risks, but being willing to step out of your comfort zone and expect that everything you need will show up.

I spent years trying to live someone else's dream. It looked like success on the outside, but inside there was always a constant battle between what I was supposed to want and what I really wanted. I was supposed to want to climb the corporate ladder, but what I really wanted was to be home with my daughter and do work that I loved – even if it meant a huge pay cut. It's one of the reasons I relocated to Minnesota: I downsized my life and was preparing to live on less so I could create the life I wanted. I was already earning six figures working as a remote employee. When else would I get the opportunity to relocate to a place of my choice without having to look for a new job?

I took a big risk in moving to Minnesota. While still living in Delaware, I contacted a group for single mothers, based in the Twin Cities, and asked them lots of questions about neighborhoods and schools. I found out the schools here tested in 2nd and 5th grade for placement in their gifted program. I planned my move a month before the testing so my daughter would be eligible. She took the test and went to magnet school for gifted kids in 3rd grade. She recently started middle school taking Honors English, writing, and history. When I compare her opportunities now to the Philadelphia schools that are cutting out music, art, and athletics, I am so glad I made the move to Minnesota.

Was it bold and ballsy to pick up my life and move halfway across the country? Absolutely. I could have stayed in Philadelphia to please everyone and ease their discomfort, but I needed to be true to what God was calling me to do. The risk was worth the reward: since making the move to Minnesota, my professional and personal life have grown tremendously. And four years later those women I connected with before I even moved here are some of my closest friends.

Are you playing it safe by avoiding all risks, or are you taking the leaps of faith that position you for more purpose, passion, and prosperity?

If you find yourself putting off what you really want to do, I challenge you to remove the word "eventually" from your vocabulary. By definition, eventually means at an unspecified future time. So if you are telling yourself that you will eventually start your business, write your book, launch that foundation, or whatever it means for you to pursue your purpose, you are setting yourself up to drift through your life as a disciplined wisher.

Trailblazers don't use the word "eventually" when describing their purpose-based passion. They set dates, milestones, and targets, even if they are tentative. Why? Because people serious about making things happen take action TODAY. Whether it's a huge leap or a small step that's preparing you for a huge leap, it's critical to your success that you take action now!

The expectation that you will "eventually" go after what you really want is the mindset of women who settle for mediocrity. But you have been given a purpose, and your purpose is not an option – it's your calling.

If you were to do a progress check on the goals you've set toward pursing your passion, would you be on target, playing catch-up, or totally off track? If you are not making the progress you expected, have you been in a holding pattern? Waiting for the perfect situation or some other mythical milestone?

Lots of people say they want to be a trailblazer, but what they forget is that in order to blaze a trail you have to be willing to bear the torch and keep it lit.

Who's your role model? Is it Barbara Corcoran, Iyanla Vanzant, Sarah Blakely, Bill and Melinda Gates, Tony Robbins, or Oprah? Maybe it is someone with a name less recognized, but with no less impact on the lives of the people they reach. The people that inspire us are usually trailblazers; they took a leap of faith when others couldn't or refused to see. They were bold, they were tenacious, and they were committed. Chances are they were doubted, often discouraged, and misunderstood, too.

I read an article about Oprah and the impact of her starting the OWN Network. The author of the article said Oprah missed the mark by going off-brand, and it caused her to slip on the Forbes Most Powerful Women List from #6 to #50. The article went on to say that her jump to cable also cost her a huge chunk of her audience. I had a different perspective.

Oprah is a trailblazer and pioneer. She could have stayed in the box of other people's expectations. But by pursuing her vision, she modeled what being willing to step into something new looks like, even if it means having to step back later and reconfigure. Often when you are trying something new, the only model you have is the one you are creating as you go. How many other women have launched a television network in the last 50 years? How many African-American women have launched a television network in the last 100 years?

Sure, Oprah could have played it safe, but she CHOSE to blaze another trail, take bigger risks, and make and learn from new mistakes. If you choose to blaze a trail, know that not everyone will follow. In fact, you are guaranteed to have some naysayers and haters. Then there are also those of us who marvel at the boldness of your journey and the brilliance in your blaze.

3 - REFUSE TO GIVE UP WHEN YOU ENCOUNTER A SETBACK

Sometimes giving up feels like the best option after a setback.

A lay-off. Divorce. Death of a family member. Break-up of a friendship. Loss of a key member of your support system. Any of these can take you off the course leading to your purpose. Brilliant women adapt; we dig in our heels and summon our resilience. This doesn't mean that we don't feel pain; it just means that we refuse to let our emotions dictate our choices and responses.

I had everything planned out for how I was going to break free from corporate America. I was happily building my business online, picking up new clients, and getting local speaking gigs. Things were looking good.

And. Then. It. Happened.

I was sidetracked by a divorce that took a toll emotionally, financially, and physically – I was completely drained. In the midst of the legalities of divorce I was trying to manage a day job, hang on to my side business (which I was loving), and take care of my daughter and myself. Something had to give, right?

I ended up taking a step back with my coaching business. I took some time to regroup, relocate, and, more importantly, rest. Though

I was still strong in my desire to leave my day job, the change in my lifestyle after the divorce made that dream seem out of reach. Knowing that the sorrow of not pursuing one's purpose is more costly than the discomfort of stepping out on faith, I refused to give up on what I really wanted.

The most valuable lesson lived from that period of my life is that desire is different than motivation. Just because you want to do something (change careers, launch your business, go after a promotion), that doesn't always mean you have the motivation to take action. Many of us get lost in that fine line between hoping something will happen and making things happen. Motivation is the compass that helps us choose the way back to our goals.

If you feel like you're off track, now is the perfect time for you to gather your thoughts and move forward again. The first step is to reconnect to the source of your motivation. Here are my other suggestions for getting back in the game:

- Re-establish your vision. Figure out where you want to be. What do you want in your life? What matters most to you right now and where do you want to go from here? Take the time to visualize your dream life. Try to envision as many details as you can so you can get a sense of what it will feel like when you accomplish your goals.
- Write your vision down. Focus on what you do want rather than what you don't have or don't want. Put all of this information down on paper in a format that works for you, such as a mind map or a brainstorm cloud. You need to be able to process this information after you jot it down on paper.
- Review your current goals. How do your current goals and aspirations relate to your dream life? Are you setting specific goals for the vision you have? If not, then revise your goals

so they're in line with your purpose. Remember: your goals are only effective if they're driving you toward your vision. Anything else is just busy work.

- Create visual representations of your goals. Keeping your goals in the forefront of your mind is essential to developing the motivation to see them through to fruition. Place reminders for yourself on note cards, sticky notes, poster boards, dry erase boards, and anywhere else that you'll see them and be able to think about them. This is the perfect time to create a vision board.
- Enlist help and support. Surround yourself with loved ones who support you and your goals. They'll be some of the best help for rediscovering your motivation. Cherish and appreciate the people who motivate you, cheer you on, and feed you positive energy at every turn.
- Stay focused. Remind yourself constantly of why your vision is important. Close your eyes and visualize the people you are meant to serve and the impact you will have on their lives. When the "why" of your vision is clear, it's easier for you to stay motivated, even when challenges cross your path.
- Go on a mental diet. Eliminate what does not nurture your soul. Everything from what you watch, to what you hear, to the conversations you have. Consciously feed on messages that rejuvenate your spirit.

If you can move past your feelings and dig deep to restore your motivation – you may find that your seeming derailment is the perfect catalyst for the success you want.

4 - BE HAPPY FOR OTHER PEOPLE'S SUCCESS

According to the Urban Dictionary, a "hater" can be defined as:

- A person who feels anger and/or jealousy for someone who has succeeded in something they have worked hard for.
- A being that speaks badly, and/or takes negative actions in an attempt to create problems for a successful person.

Clearly, being a "hater" is not a good thing. And how we handle other people's success, especially when things may not be going so well for us, is an indicator of our maturity and belief in ourselves.

So what do you do when you see someone thriving with the opportunities, recognition, clients, and wins that you want for your life or business? You learn to celebrate other people's success.

If you master generating genuine happiness for other people, not only will you find a cure for the envy, which can sabotage your success, but there are additional benefits as well. Here's what you open the door to as you welcome and express joy for others:

- Freedom from frustration and worry. When you see another person's win as a loss for you, you pave the way for discouragement and resentment to set in. Instead, allow

- other people's success to ignite hope for the success coming in your time of harvest.
- More opportunities to be happy! Rejoicing with others creates an opportunity to multiply the good times you get to celebrate. By seizing every chance to sincerely congratulate others on their success, you are creating an atmosphere for others to be willing to celebrate your successes.
- Improved relationships with others. Healthy relationships involve sharing both ups and downs. People are more likely to respond positively to you if they sense that you're truly happy for them.
- Good karma. You reap what you sow. Giving unselfishly creates a win for everybody.

I know, it all sounds good, but how do you actually pull it off -- and do it sincerely? Here are six ideas:

1. Proactively look for opportunities to shine a spotlight on someone else. Keep in touch with what's going on in the lives of the people around you. Others may be bashful about mentioning their own victories, but still appreciate having their efforts recognized.
2. Create a daily gratitude list. It's difficult to be happy for other people when you are dissatisfied with your life. Remind yourself of all the wonderful things you have to be grateful for. Go one step better and share one thing a day with someone.
3. Be aware of your jealousy. Weigh the consequences of jealousy and envy. Be honest with yourself when you notice your thoughts and feelings heading down a negative path.
4. "Fake it till you make it." Or as Karen Salmansohn says, "Faith it till you make it." It's okay to use some artificial gestures to get started. Even if you're not purely happy

that your ex-husband got an award, you can say something gracious.
5. Start with the people you love. Charity starts at home and so should the celebration. It might be difficult to get instantly excited about the lives of strangers. However, you can start by focusing on the people closest to you. For example, cheer with enthusiasm when your cousin wins an award, your brother gets a promotion, or a friend successfully closes a deal.
6. Work your way up to dealing with the hard stuff. For example, celebrating with someone who got something you wanted for yourself or being happy for someone you believe is undeserving.

With practice, you'll be able to tackle the more sensitive issues. When you find the techniques that work with the people you love, you can use those same strategies with more challenging opportunities.

So the next time someone you know gets great news, don't hate -- celebrate with them. Remember, you reap what you sow: you can look forward to welcoming more joy into your own life as you celebrate other people's success.

5 - COMMIT TO PURSUING YOUR PURPOSE

"The moment you commit and quit holding back, all sorts of unforeseen incidents, meetings, and material assistance will rise up to help you. The simple act of commitment is a powerful magnet for help." — Napoleon Hill

Many people believe the opposite of success is failure. It's not. The opposite of success is giving up. The antidote to giving up and the key to successfully pursuing your passion-based purpose is your commitment.

Brilliant women commit to:

- Being authentic, accountable, and in integrity when it comes to their life and work.
- Studying successful role models to learn what to do and what not to do.
- Being willing to do what other people won't as their standard, not an exception.
- Stepping out of their comfort zone and taking risks.
- Practicing faith and staying spiritually grounded in every season of life.
- Being a cheerleader for their vision and a champion of other visionaries.
- Nurturing a healthy mindset towards wealth and success.

- Learning from mistakes and finding opportunities in failures.
- Planning, measuring, and revising their goals as needed.
- Investing wisely in personal and professional development.
- Maximizing their productivity with the right systems, support, and tools.
- Acknowledging and removing whatever doesn't get results.
- Celebrating their success and the success of others.
- Doing the work of becoming.

What commitments do you need to make to ensure that you stand firm in the face of challenges, obstacles, and setbacks? Choose from the commitments or make your own. Turn them into affirmations that you reflect on before you go to bed and before you start your day.

IT'S TIME TO RECLAIM YOUR BRILLIANCE

The women who have been the most influential in my life are women who chose to reclaim their brilliance. They are women who have endured painful pasts. They are women who made a courageous decision to move beyond just surviving to thriving. They are women who intentionally sow into the lives of others. They are women who have shifted from pain to purpose.

I wish I had met them sooner. I also know that they appeared when I was ready. And I am so grateful that they showed up and so generously sowed their light into my life. Their being willing to live in their purpose opened the doors and windows that have allowed me to find my way.

A few years ago I attended a retreat in Hinkley, MN, with ten other women. It was a time for us to have some solitude away from our home offices so we could focus on specific projects, as well as a time to connect. At the time I was working a full-time job and managing social media as a part-time business. My intention was to get up-to-date on my blogging.

I shared a roomed with Betty Liedtke. As we were getting ready for bed, she began to tell me about her travels to Uganda and the dream work she did with women. She also told me about a woman named

Tabitha from Uganda. Somehow we started talking about a few of the stories that I share in this book. I didn't mention it to her, but I had a strong sense that I would be doing some work with her and the women in Uganda. It was a passing feeling and I don't think I even mentioned it to her.

Some months later I joined Women of Words, a local group of women writers. Betty was there and we casually reconnected. I bought her book and was excited to learn about another trip she was preparing to take to Uganda.

During this time, I was really struggling to connect to my purpose. I was good at a lot of things. I had lots of passions, too. Although social media management was easy for me to write about and teach, it wasn't what made my heart feel connected to God. I began coaching again. My coaching would start off focused on marketing, but the conversations always led back to helping the person connect the dots between their purpose and passion. I began to realize that the problem with marketing wasn't about the tools or the tactics they were using – it was about being connected to the message they were sending. Their message needed to be grounded in purpose.

So I shifted my business to begin helping women (and some men, too) connect to their passion-based purpose. I started using my skills as an instructional designer to help them turn their expertise and experience into products, courses, and programs. I worked with them to create workshops, coaching programs, and home study courses that would allow them to reach more people, change more lives, and grow their wealth.

In August of 2012, I began piloting a live workshop focused on creating information products. Betty signed up. And she also bought a space for Tabitha, who was now living in Minnesota. It was just the two of them in the workshop that day; a third person had been unable to attend. During a break, Tabitha told me that when I walked into the room, something in her spirit told her I was the one that she needed to help her. That day, I helped her outline a woman's leadership program that would be taken back to Uganda.

Stepping into my purpose was about to create a ripple all the way to Uganda. I was reminded of that nudge in my spirit that night Betty and I first began talking. I was humbled and grateful to have the opportunity to use my gifts and sow my light into another brilliant soul. I thought about how this opportunity would have been missed had I been unwilling to pursue my purpose. Or how if I hadn't had the courage to move to Minnesota in the first place, I would never have met Betty. Or how if Betty hadn't stepped out of her comfort zone and into her purpose, she would never have met Tabitha or gone to Uganda.

See, there really are people who can't step into their purpose until you step into yours. And you can't fully step into your purpose until you reclaim your brilliance and break free from eclipse living.

Who's Waiting For You?

Who is waiting for you to show up and be exactly who you were created to be? Not a dimly lit spirit, with your brilliance eclipsed by pain, resentment, and bitterness, but a brilliant soul, abundantly flowing in love and grace.

I envision a world where every woman is ablaze with passion and purpose, and prosperously sowing into the world. Creating ripples of transformation in the women, men, children, families, and communities they serve. I see women leading with their light, instead of trudging along with hearts full of complacency and fear. Imagine the impact. Imagine the unlimited potential. Imagine the revolution.

My prayer is that you know in the depths of your soul, without a shadow of a doubt, that you are here for a purpose. And that instead of allowing pain from your past to shackle you to fear and shame, you allow it to be a catalyst for the brilliance you were meant to share with the world.

It's time to reclaim your brilliance.

ABOUT THE AUTHOR

Believing that the lessons we live divinely position us to sow into the lives others, Tai Goodwin boldly speaks about finding the courage to live and speak your truth. Her own life's lessons have come from first-hand experience of abuse, dysfunction, and divorce. In 2009, she made a life-changing decision. She left everything she knew behind and moved half way across the country to Minnesota on a mission to create a better life for herself and her daughter. Now happily remarried, her vision is to help more women see the pain of their past as facets of the brilliance they get to share with the world.

A contributor to the Huffington Post, Tai is an author, speaker, and business coach for women entrepreneurs. A champion of women supporting women, she is host of the Brilliant Business Girlfriends Podcast. A former teacher, Tai's professional history includes time at two Fortune 500 companies before making her own transition from employee to entrepreneur. An award-winning instructional designer, Tai is certified in human performance improvement. She has a B.S. and M.S. in education and over 19 years of experience in learning & development.